Collapse at Meuse-Argonne

Collapse at Meuse-Argonne

The Failure of the Missouri-Kansas Division

Robert H. Ferrell

University of Missouri Press
Columbia

Copyright © 2004 by
The Curators of the University of Missouri
University of Missouri Press, Columbia, Missouri 65211
Printed and bound in the United States of America
All rights reserved
First paperback printing, 2017

Library of Congress Cataloging-in-Publication Data

Ferrell, Robert H.
Collapse at Meuse-Argonne : the failure of the Missouri-Kansas
Division / Robert H. Ferrell.
p. cm.
Includes bibliographical references and index.
ISBN–13: 978-0-8262-2142-1 (paperback : alk. paper)
1. Argonne, Battle of the, France, 1918. 2. United States.
Army. Division, 35th. 3. World War, 1914–1918—Regimental
histories—United States. I. Title.
D545.A63F47 2004
940.4´36—dc22

                                        2004004300

Designer: Kristie Lee
Typefaces: Adobe Garamond, Schneidler MedT Bold

In memory of PFC Ernest H. Ferrell, Sr. (1891–1985),
AEF defensive sector, Oise-Aisne, Meuse-Argonne

Contents

For these men plodding southward on that chill morning, there was ended a period of five days of intense activity, excitement and shock such as war alone can give—five days crowded with events that will go to make up and are even now a part of the history of the operations of the World War. The study of that period, here so briefly outlined, will some day be adequately described and added to the works that tell of conflicts of armed men—a vast library in which delve students of military history, soldiers anxious to profit by the experience of others.

— ROBERT H. FLETCHER JR., "The 35th Division in the First Phase of the Meuse-Argonne Operation, September 26–October 1, 1918," Infantry School, Fort Benning, Georgia, 1923-1924, file 235-18.2, box 3, Thirty-fifth Division historical, entry 1241, Record Group 120, National Archives, College Park, Maryland

Preface

It is always a pleasant task to write of a winning military unit or commander. The defeats, and there have been many in American history and indeed in the history of all nations, are less pleasant, especially when they involve, as did that of the Thirty-fifth (Missouri-Kansas) Division in World War I in the battle of the Meuse-Argonne, a high-minded, hardworking group that deserved to win. The Thirty-fifth contained men with a future. The most remarkable in that respect was Captain Harry S. Truman of Battery D of the 129th Field Artillery Regiment. Major Dwight F. Davis, adjutant of the division's Sixty-ninth Brigade, became secretary of war in the administration of President Calvin Coolidge and was perhaps better known as the donor of the Davis Cup in tennis. Major Bennett Champ Clark would serve as U.S. senator from Missouri. The division's YMCA head, Henry J. Allen, was a notable progressive in Kansas politics, a close friend of William Allen White of the *Emporia Gazette,* and was elected governor of his state in 1918. Several of the principal officers of the division, two of them regimental commanders, were admirable figures. The commander of the 139th Infantry Regiment, a National Guard officer, Lieutenant Colonel Carl L. Ristine, a remarkably handsome former football player at the University of Missouri, possessed verve and intelligence. His was a leadership any regiment could admire. Commanding the 140th Infantry was Lieutenant Colonel Channing E. Delaplane, a Regular Army officer, a figure to remember if only because of his facial features, which resembled those of a bulldog; "Dogface Delaplane" was his sobriquet, and he knew of it and was proud of it. He was the only regimental colonel who kept his regiment together until the last day of the action. Of the battalion commanders there was Major Joseph E.

Rieger, whom Brigadier General Lucien G. Berry pronounced "absolutely impossible." Rieger was a tall, gaunt lawyer from Kirksville, Missouri, of a religious bent, who at Camp Doniphan in Oklahoma organized a Sunday school that enrolled three hundred members. General Berry doubtless hated him for that reason, not to mention the fact that he was a Guard officer. But when a remnant of the division, after the fiercest of fights, reached the village of Exermont in the Meuse-Argonne, the farthest point the division gained (and then lost), Rieger was in the group of heroes who made it into the village and a bit beyond.

The Thirty-fifth did not deserve to lose, but it did. Its collapse was a saddening episode in American military history. But there is much to learn from its failure, for it showed how tenuous was the victory of the American Expeditionary Forces (AEF) in France in the World War of now nearly a century ago; how difficult were the challenges; how the men of the AEF did the best they could and, despite such defeats as that of the Thirty-fifth Division, in the end won through to victory.

Acknowledgments

All books need assistance, and in the present instance I am indebted to friends at the National Archives in College Park, Maryland, especially the branch chief of modern military records, Timothy K. Nenninger, and the World War I specialist, Mitchell Yockelson. Both pointed out files to investigate and read chapters in draft. At the U.S. Army Military History Institute, Army War College, Carlisle Barracks, Carlisle, Pennsylvania, help came from the head of the search room, Richard J. Sommers, and archivist David A. Keough. At the Harry S. Truman Library in Independence, Missouri, librarian Elizabeth Safly and archivists Randy Sowell and Dennis E. Bilger. At the Liberty Memorial in Kansas City, archivist Jonathan R. Casey and curator Doran L. Cart. My thanks also to the staff of the Kansas State Historical Society in Topeka.

Friends do special things, such as John Hulston, lawyer of Springfield, Missouri, and a ready resource on Missouri history; John Lukacs and John Cooper, who read the manuscript; and Dennis Giangreco, who offered his conference paper on Captain Harry S. Truman of the 129th Field Artillery Regiment. Larry I. Bland provided a copy of the diary of Pierpont L. Stackpole. David K. Frasier and Jeffrey C. Graf, of the Indiana University Library in Bloomington, provided answers to arcane questions. Louise Malcomb found fugitive congressional documents.

Betty Bradbury was the word processor; John M. Hollingsworth, the cartographer.

A thank-you, again, to the director of the University of Missouri Press, Beverly Jarrett, for her interest in the book and her readings, and to the press's managing editor, Jane Lago, who expertly edited the manuscript.

And to Carolyn and Lorin, who make everything easier.

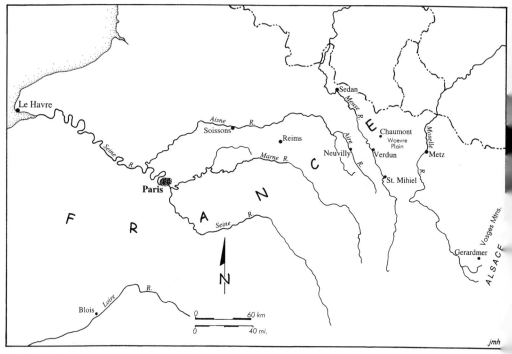

Northern France.

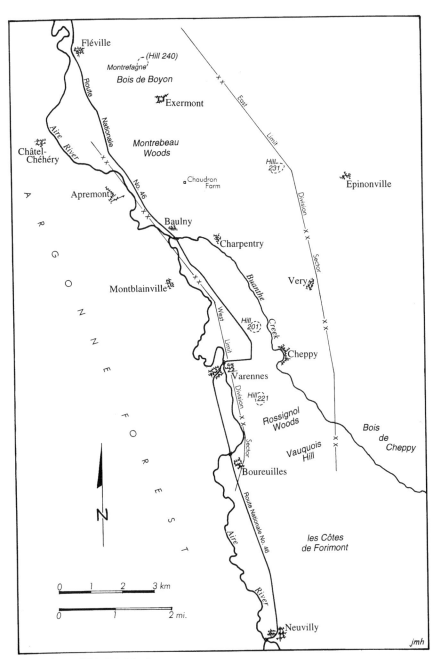

The Thirty-fifth Division's sector.

Collapse at Meuse-Argonne

One

Preparation

The Thirty-fifth Division of the U.S. Army got into trouble—the division collapsed and had to be taken out of the line—during the first days of the battle of the Meuse-Argonne in 1918. The question is, How this could have happened? The men surely were good enough, these 28,000 soldiers, members of National Guard units from Missouri and Kansas combined into one division (14,287 were from Missouri, and 9,781 from Kansas, with the rest being mostly draftees from the two states). General John J. Pershing told the division's commander that without any disparagement of any other division of the American Expeditionary Forces he considered the Missouri-Kansas division the "best looking lot of men I have got in France," superb candidates for fighting the forces of Imperial Germany.[1] At the outset the division was commanded by Major General William M. Wright, who later as commanding general of the Eighty-ninth Division presided over one of the four best AEF divisions; the Eighty-ninth was one of the two point divisions in the final, and immensely successful, attack in the Meuse on November 1, which rolled up the German opponents and may have been the Allied blow that brought an end to the awful war that opened in August 1914.

With such splendid human material, and a competent trainer of men in warfare, something went wrong, and the question is what.

I

It is a bromide of historical analysis to relate that some issue is complicated, that for this or that result there are several reasons, and then to let the reader agree with that conclusion, which after all is nothing more than a truism. The truism holds for this case, yet one must say that a signal reason in the combination that broke the Thirty-fifth Division was poor training.

The division's units—brigades, regiments, battalions, companies—came together for the first time in September 1917, when a tent camp opened at Camp Doniphan within the Fort Sill reservation in Oklahoma. From across the reaches of Missouri and Kansas, from the farms and towns and the two major Missouri metropolises of St. Louis and Kansas City, arrived the somewhat bedraggled National Guard units that were entering federal service. Perhaps their Guard origin was one of the factors in the poor training that followed. Regular Army officers would speak often of the division as "a National Guard division" and therefore, they implied, undisciplined and impervious to discipline. By that they meant that the men showed little respect for their officers and lacked the snap and polish, the ability to salute smartly and not question orders, that Regular Army troops displayed. In some measure this was true. The Guard did have the political background so often pointed out by the Regulars, especially West Pointers who felt that anyone who had not been to West Point knew nothing of the military arts. Guard troops assembled every two weeks for close-order drill and once a year attended summer camp, a week or two of nearly unadulterated fun. Harry S. Truman, a farmer near Grandview, Missouri, joined the Guard in 1905, when he was twenty-one years old (his parents, with Confederate sympathies, would not have allowed him to join before he came of age), and wrote to his cousins in Independence that during one of the camps it rained so much that the ground was covered with water, and the men dug holes so that officers would fall into them. Truman spent two enlistments, six years, in the Missouri Guard and achieved the rank of corporal. Another problem with the Guard, apart from its capacity for fun rather than military wisdom, was that in Guard units the men elected their officers, which put leadership on a basis of popularity. The Guard, one almost has to conclude, was not a good foundation for a division that would enter a serious European war.[2]

The Guard had a little experience prior to the declaration of war, and that was along the Mexican border. It impressed a lad of seventeen in Sedalia,

Missouri, William S. Triplet, who lied about his age to get into the Guard in 1917 and whose reason for entering apart from the opportunity for adventure was that his school principal promised a diploma to all volunteers, and young Triplet was failing a class in German. Although he never received the high school diploma, he did encounter the border veterans, who appeared once his company arrived at Camp Doniphan. The veterans impressed the youngster, especially with their stories, most of which were improbable.[3] In fact, the border was no more of a training experience than the drills in Sedalia. Troops spent several boring months there in the sand and dirt, principally maintaining themselves, while six thousand Regulars under Brigadier General Pershing went into northern Mexico in a vain search for the ragtag troops of the Mexican renegade Pancho Villa.

Real training, such as it was, began on October 1 after the Guard arrived in camp. Alas, some of it was based on Cuban and Philippine experiences, rather than on those of Europe's armies.

Here it is necessary to say that the U.S. Army, the Regular Army, on April 1, 1917, consisted of 5,791 officers and 131,797 enlisted men. The rolls of the National Guard listed an additional 181,620 officers and men, of whom 80,446 had been called to federal service. The U.S. Army stood seventeenth in numerical estimates of the world's armies, behind that of Portugal. It had no experience of modern war. The last of the Civil War veterans, Colonel John Clem, who had been a drummer boy in the great war of 1861–1865, retired in 1915. The Indian fighters were much in evidence, a prime example being the army's chief of staff, Major General Hugh L. Scott, who was accustomed to showing visitors his collection of Indian headdresses and relating the importance of the individual feathers. Most of the officers, and a few of the men, had been in the Spanish-American War, that conflict where the principal campaign was against the Spanish-held port of Santiago. For this attack the army fielded 27,000 men, less than the size of a division in World War I.[4] Many officers had seen service during the Filipino insurrection, a series of small engagements in jungle country that went on for years after the Peace of Paris of 1898. The army also assisted with pacifications in a few Central American and Caribbean countries.

In the training of the Guard units of the Thirty-fifth there was a marked inattention to what had been happening in Europe. The guns of August 1914, which inaugurated the historical twentieth century—even though the nineteenth century ended numerically on December 31, 1899—were far distant from the officers and the garrison army of the United States whose camps and posts spread, usually by political design, across the country. The army sent officers to observe the fighting in Europe, some of them assigned to the German Army, but the reports of those officers came back to Washington only to be unread. In 1915 an officer or two began to look at the pile, but a jurisdictional dispute arose in which the dispatches finally were allotted to the president of the War College in Washington, who was to disseminate anything that it was possible to draw from them. That officer did little or nothing with what might have been prime knowledge.[5]

The European war was far removed from the officers who instructed the Thirty-fifth Division, and they could trust only the manuals for training that the War Department in Washington sent to the field. The manuals were not fascinating reading, and were careful in their conclusions. They acknowledged the existence of war in Europe and instructed readers to learn the details of trench warfare, for, they asserted, the European war in 1914–1917 was fought from an array of trenches.

Thus, officers in training positions across the country in the dozens of cantonments emphasized trench warfare. But that was not what the men were going to encounter in France. They would discover, belatedly, that most of the training was useless—Sergeant Triplet years later, when he was a graduate of West Point, a retired Regular colonel who had been up for brigadier general at the end of World War II, never believed his World War I platoon in the Thirty-fifth was untrained, but that was not true of most of the units of the division. Triplet was smart and did all right in the Argonne with his platoon of fifty men, part of the 140th Infantry Regiment. Unfortunately the 140th was the only regiment in the Thirty-fifth that held together, and he was unable to see what happened to the others under the training that the Regular officers gave them. It was totally unimaginative, considering that the German Army, the best trained army in the world, at that time was going over to a new concept of war, using *Stellungen,* or positions, rather than trenches. This involved shrewd placing of machine-gun nests, with reserves behind, and support by well-sited artillery batteries, and in the attack a subtle mixing of annihilating artillery fire with groups of trained troops that bypassed strong points in favor of moving through lines to the back areas where they could spread destruction and turn order into chaos. These were, indeed, the tactical dispositions of World War II. The only things lacking were effective tanks (the tanks of World War I were so primitive and slow that they were of very limited use, moving at only five or six miles an hour, lightly armored, with inside temperatures of 120 degrees

Fahrenheit or more, armed with 30-caliber machine guns or 37-mm one-pounder guns) and planes that could effectively rake troops with machine guns and heavy explosives.

The Allied armies, those of Great Britain and France, which in 1917 were barely managing to hold the front lines, were without knowledge that the German Army was changing its tactical dispositions and believed that what had prevailed, trench warfare, would continue; perhaps for that reason the Americans could be forgiven for believing the same. Not long after the American declaration of war, the British and French sent military missions to Washington, and their advice to the American military was to prepare the new divisions about to be raised so that those masses of men, to be trained beginning in the autumn, would know how to act when they arrived in the trenches and took up their portion of the line. Pershing went over to France with a small group of officers in May 1917, and among his initial inquiries that summer was whether the War Department in Washington had translated French manuals for dissemination to commanders and troops, once training began. The department replied that it had translated twenty-three manuals and would see to their dissemination.

After the war the War College undertook a study of tactics in the AEF, and one of its first ambitious projects was to make a study of the Thirty-fifth Division's training and performance.[6] Here it is evident that trench warfare was what the men of the Thirty-fifth encountered in training. Members of the Allied missions to Washington had stressed the importance of the trenches. Some of them were heard to say that trench warfare had come to stay, superseding the older forms; they remarked, seriously, that if the Allied armies ever reached Berlin it would be from trench to trench. This influence in the summer of 1917 was probably controlling. In any event, the War Department accepted the doctrine and on August 26 issued training bulletin number 656, entitled "Infantry Training." The first sentence read: "In all the military training of a division, under existing conditions, training for trench warfare is of paramount importance." The second paragraph made one of the first duties of a division commander the laying out of a trench system, to be constructed without delay and used as the focus of all training.[7]

Nothing if not organized, the War Department system of training provided for a complete organization of schools, dealing with all specialties. The instruction of troops was to take place over sixteen weeks. This in turn was to be only the first period of training. The second period offered general instructions, to continue in more detail the work begun in the first. The War College investigators searched a large miscellany of papers in the adjutant general's office. Not only those of divisions but also those of higher headquarters, corps and army and General Headquarters, came back from France in a terrible confusion, and some of them, important papers, doubtless never turned up. They managed, however, almost by a miracle, to find a series of weekly drill schedules for the Thirty-fifth, covering a period of fifteen weeks, from October 8, 1917, to January 19, 1918. The only schedule not found was probably that for the first week. It was clear that the division trained in close accordance with the War Department program set out in bulletin 656.

The first inspection of the division was made by an inspector from the inspector general's office, Colonel F. M. Caldwell, between November 24 and December 7, and consisted of two weeks of careful combing of what the division was about. The War Department schedule at that time was only halfway finished. Caldwell was much impressed with the men individually. He rated their physique as "excellent" and the average of intelligence as "high." He was less satisfied with the way in which the human material was handled. But perhaps it was too early for him to have been sure of very much.[8]

The commander of the Thirty-fifth at that time, General Wright, and the division chief of staff were not present to speak with Colonel Caldwell, as they were in France. Pershing had asked the War Department to bring over the highest officers to let them see what the front looked like, and when they went to the British part of the front the commander in chief asked for evaluations from their hosts, some of which were not complimentary. A few of the division generals were obviously tired and sleepy-minded, past their primes if they ever had been in them. The ambitious and politically sensitive and very able Major General Leonard Wood, a former chief of staff, was in the group, and Wood was not bashful in offering his opinions, so much so that later there ensued a contretemps in which Secretary of War Newton D. Baker, with the backing of President Woodrow Wilson and, in the background, Pershing himself, denied Wood the privilege of taking the well-trained Eighty-ninth Division to Europe and relegated him to an administrative command in San Francisco; it was this arrangement that permitted Wright, after holding several corps commands, nominal posts at that time, to take the Eighty-ninth.

As head of the Thirty-fifth, Wright went over with the other generals,

and the Thirty-fifth was under temporary command of its artillery brigadier, General Lucien G. Berry, the nemesis of the then Lieutenant Truman,
who described him with special malice as an old fuddy-duddy who, when
angered, which was often, rattled his false teeth at opponents. Berry brought
up Truman for promotion to captain but kept him and two other lieutenants standing outside a mess hall for an hour or two in the intense Camp
Doniphan cold, which forced Truman to miss reveille the next morning,
and meanwhile grilled him, shouting at him that like all lieutenants he
knew nothing, could know nothing. (When the lieutenants arrived in France
it was to learn that they all had been promoted.)9 Berry was an uncertain,
one must say unskilled, artillery commander who at the beginning of the
Meuse-Argonne did not believe in airplane spotting of German guns and
told anyone who would listen, including a young lieutenant from the corps
inspector general's office, who recommended Berry's relief, that planes were
"no damn good."10 Berry's presiding over the drill schedule could hardly have
been a plus, although there is no evidence that Caldwell noticed his un-
suitability.

General Wright returned from his European trip in December, and it is
uncertain what he brought back, beyond what was plainly visible—trench
warfare. The great German spring offensives were to commence with the
massive onslaught of March 21, 1918, in which everything about trench warfare became plainly obsolete. When abroad Wright and the other commanding generals were hearing rumbles of Pershing's unhappiness with British
and French instruction. The commander in chief had been absurdly busy in
the preceding months, for he had to organize his headquarters, at the old
French garrison town of Chaumont, from the very foundation. He also had
to arrange a sector where his troops coming over in the spring—only the
First, Second, Twenty-sixth, and Forty-second divisions arrived prior to that
time—could be bivouacked and, he began to say, trained. In addition to
such tasks, Pershing was beyond question one of the U.S. Army's most de-
voted micromanagers. He could not avoid getting himself into any and all
details; wanted everything, pertinent to his high office or not, sent up to
him; and spent his days sitting in his ornate Paris residence, or as soon as he
could his Chaumont office, chewing tobacco and using a rubber tree or two
in the office as a spittoon.

Thus, even with all else he had to do, Pershing did not fail to become involved in the details of tactical doctrine involving the training of the troops
under his command. He had allowed his artillery commander, Major

General Peyton C. March, to return to the United States as army chief of staff, and at first presumed that March would do his every bidding. When he discovered that March, who was a first-class administrator, would not, he tangled with March over troop training, among many other subjects. When Wright was in France the commanding general of the Thirty-fifth could hear rumbles of what would become open contention between Pershing and March over what Pershing said was the un-American (by which he meant British and French) training of troops in the United States. He especially criticized the trench-minded nature of the training. Pershing was saying that American principles of fighting could not be those of foreign armies—Americans were resolute soldiers and wished to advance, not to defend a trench. The AEF demanded to fight in its own way, not like the effete, stalemate-devoted, armies of Britain and France. The War College study of 1921–1922 was careful in making its point about what was clearly a growing divergence of doctrine between the nation's two four-star generals, Pershing and March, although Pershing assumed that he was the senior commander. During the European trip Wright and the others learned that there was a "tendency . . . in discussions among officers to depart from this sound doctrine," the latter being Pershing's doctrine of getting troops out of trenches and into open warfare. A memorandum given Wright and the others explicitly denied that there had been a change in the principles of combat and held up as the "ultimate object of all trench operations . . . warfare in the open conducted in all essential elements according to the principles found in our standard manuals."[11]

When the visiting commanders returned they could see a divergence in ideas about training, but each acted, wrote the War College officers looking into the Thirty-fifth in their study, upon the information "according to his own individual judgment."[12] Officially, home training was still governed by bulletin 656 and similar manuals.

By April 1918, when the Thirty-fifth was about to go overseas, the commander in chief at Chaumont was sure of what earlier he had been intimating. "Too much trench warfare works against the success of great operations," he cabled. "Men so trained when brought into the open have a feeling of nakedness and helplessness."[13]

This was at the least an interesting change of mind, whatever its origins—perhaps rivalry with General March, who had taken over administration of the War Department, virtually relegating Secretary Baker to insignificance, and was willing to take over management of the rear areas of the AEF in

France. It appeared to display a remarkable prescience. The German spring and summer offensives were in course, and Pershing's caution in the winter might have changed into certitude as he saw the Allied lines nearly buckle against the extraordinary new German tactics. It is not very clear, however, what sort of dedication to open warfare Pershing was displaying. When he advised against trench warfare in the April 1918 cable mentioned above, he added two sentences that took back most of what he advocated: "Recommend, for infantry, musketry, close order drill, minor tactics in open warfare situations. For field artillery, driving, care of horses."

And so most of Pershing's divisions coming over, thirty-eight of them out of his ultimate command of forty-two, with twenty-nine in the line during the long, cruel weeks of the Meuse-Argonne, were trained for trench warfare. Their commanders, uncertain after their introduction to the fighting in France in the early winter of 1917, returned to find the divisions mostly trained and could only visit their confusion upon them.

2

In the Thirty-fifth Division it was difficult to see deviation from the bulletin numbered 656. The division's history mentioned several schools operated at this time, one for platoon commanders, emphasizing discipline and precision, the "click of heels," and so on. In retrospect it sounds silly. We do know that when an inspector went over the division after it came off the line on October 1, in disarray, he deplored—Regular that he was—the lack of discipline, how company-grade officers, captains and lower, gave little or no attention to saluting and fraternized with the men, while field-grade officers, majors and up, looked on with benign indifference. The division had "the National Guard mentality," the inspector agreed. Evidently the platoon school produced very poor scholarship. There was a school for company commanders, making points about leadership and command, which must have been platitudes to the Guard officers who knew their men as fellow citizens of the Republic. Interestingly, there was one large school receiving particular notice in the division history, a liaison school, instituted on February 1, 1918, with three thousand students. The War College study unfortunately offers no information as to the curriculum in liaison, knowledge of which, as the following pages will show, marked one of the most unfortunate lapses of the division when it fought in the line for its five fateful days.

In March, much time went to marching, which culminated in a march by the entire division on April 2. It covered eight miles, quite a distance for men in seventy-pound packs with bedrolls in an inverted U-shape. During the march, attention was given to training the troops in minor tactics, namely, patrolling and maintenance of communications. General Wright issued a bulletin at the end of the day giving his impression. He noted delays in starting and confusion in the trains, the accompanying baggage carried by horses and trucks, including ammunition and rolling kitchens. He did not like the work of the signal battalion, which work would lead to grave difficulties in the line in France, where the battalion's men became stretcher bearers. The marching was slow, with elongation of the columns. Patrolling followed models out of manuals and gave no attention to the ground. The division failed to keep to the prescribed road and failed to maintain advance guard distances, all with unnecessary noise and shouting.

The War College study said Wright's analysis gave the impression of "an awkward, unwieldy body on the road." To the authors of the study it seemed incredible that the division commander in his last paragraph expressed himself fairly well satisfied with the scene his division created.[14] About the only explanation one can make for that is that he knew his division was not ready for much fighting if it could not even march down a good American road, but then he had so recently returned from Europe where only four American divisions were present and where he and his fellow generals had heard a certain confusion between how the War Department advised them to train their troops and what the commander in chief was hinting at—namely, that the War Department was relying too much on foreign advice, not sticking to American principles of war, whatever they were.

There is a glimmer of preparation for open warfare in the discovery of a memo by Wright commenting on the division's instruction (the War College could not find anything specific about the instruction) in regard to war in the field, out of the trenches. This was a circular the commanding general issued a week before division headquarters left for the port of embarkation. The principal criticism of the divisional preparation was "a total lack of appreciation of officers of the value of the ground," which resembled his reaction to the day of the ragged march when some units attempted patrolling. Wright said there was an "inclination to take a normal formation and advance at a slow walk," as if the units involved had been told by their officers to perform a sort of—to them—ballet, and they did it without enthusiasm. He also noted a lack of combat reconnaissance and lack of knowledge of machine guns.[15] In the later history of the division these two latter delinquencies might have come back to haunt them, if the men and officers had looked back to remember them—but evidently the report disappeared in the enthusiasm of everyone to get on the way "over there."

Wright may have thought that when the Thirty-fifth got to France it could discover what Pershing had in mind that differed from the bulletin of the preceding August and adjust its training—he knew that Pershing desired to have special training for all his divisions. In theory, each division arriving in France was supposed to have three months of training, with the first phase including the instruction of small units; the second, training in line, preferably in a quiet sector, brigaded with an older unit; and the third, work in a training area correcting deficiencies discovered and training the division as a whole primarily in open warfare. As matters turned out, about all the Thirty-fifth experienced was the second phase. Wright left the division in July for his corps commands and eventually command of the Eighty-ninth Division that fought at St. Mihiel in early September and then the Meuse-Argonne in late October and early November.

There is little evidence, therefore, that after General Wright's return from France the Thirty-fifth changed its training routines. The enrollment of three thousand men, nearly a regiment, in a school for liaison is a tantalizing suggestion of some recognition that the war in France might not be a trench war, but then it is difficult to be sure of what the teachers told their students, for liaison was a part of trench war too—men had to communicate, from the front trenches to the rear. The French word adopted during World War I could have indicated a variety of lectures that had nothing to do with the great problem of troops in open country, which is not so much keeping together as knowing who is on either side and, for commanders, being able to summon any number of troops to some place where immediately needed. Liaison of that sort was one of the Thirty-fifth's prime lacks in the Meuse-Argonne. It would be interesting to know precisely what the instruction was, but no records survive.

With that the troops entrained for Hoboken and were shipped off to France. Some traveled via Liverpool and a "dinky train" trip across England to a Channel port where they boarded a steamer to France, while others went directly there.

Thereafter training for what the men of the Thirty-fifth would meet in the Meuse-Argonne was notably inadequate, right down to the time the division entered the line a few days before the opening of the battle that took place between the Argonne forest, on the left, and the bend upward of the

Meuse River above Verdun all the way to Sedan (which city the Thirty-fifth, of course, never would see).

Theoretically much time remained during which the Thirty-fifth could have been trained to accord with Pershing's principles, the need as he wrote the War Department to keep apart from foreign ideas and explore the possibilities of using American inventiveness and tactical imagination to get the war out of the trenches. Practically speaking this type of training proved impossible, for the division almost at once began an odyssey that included a month, May–June, of brigading with British troops, during which there were virtually conducted tours of the trenches, with companies, battalions, and regiments observing how the British Army defended its part of the huge line that ran from the Channel all the way to Switzerland.[16] The division then went, in July–August, for training with the French, which meant entering the province of Alsace and after a month of training in the line taking over, under American command, a thirty-kilometer part of a quiet sector by the name of Gerardmer, after the principal town. There the men of the Thirty-fifth manned trenches and *parados,* the stepped-up observation points, and learned about the support of the line by carrying parties that came up with huge vats of food at night and brought up the ammunition. The Vosges area was a country in itself, scenic to a fault, and in looking back to their experience in the mountainous and sometimes cloudy country where both the French and the German armies rested, the men of the Thirty-fifth Division considered it a vacation.

The Vosges was a place to remember, even if the trenches in the Gerardmer sector were worth forgetting, with their no-man's-land and occasional forays to capture prisoners or annoy the German defenders. Sergeant Triplet remembered the business of taking up artillery pieces, difficult on mountain roads, and the use of mules by French artillerymen, who cut the nostrils of the animals so they could breathe easier as they pulled the guns or brought up supply wagons. In the line it was at first awkward to listen to strange sounds, which could turn into nothing at all and were often the wind rattling the elephant iron, the sheeting that kept the elements out of the crude huts in which the men had to sleep. He remembered the frightened sentries who would hear rats running around and imagine stealthy forms with coal-scuttle helmets creeping across the few dozen yards that separated the armies, readying their bayonets or trench knives to slit fine young American throats. The sentries would raise the alarm, Triplet on duty at the nearby hut or his platoon opposites down the way would fire a flare, people would start shooting indiscriminately, and the guns farther back, the artillery, would take up the alarm, flares meanwhile creating the semblance of the Fourth of July.[17]

For those not engaged in this sort of play war in the trenches, there was a picniclike relaxation on the hillsides to the rear, living in idyllic cabins long since erected by the French Army for the care and feeding of tired divisions that posted most of their men to the rear of hills and mountains where artillery could not reach. Occasionally the men would venture into the villages to the rear, where German guns lobbed shells at regular intervals and where once a kindly woman, in words of French that did not register, warned a party of soldiers that it was time for the shell and Triplet and a friend gave no attention until they found themselves running for their lives, they thought.

Once in a while the Vosges front livened up, as Captain Truman knew from a not delightful experience. American generals felt that the French advice—to wit, that it was not a good idea to stir the German defenders: "be nice to them and they will be nice to you"—was not the American way of war. The Thirty-fifth Division instructed its artillery brigade to send a bouquet of gas shells to the German defenders, and Truman and his fellow battery commanders did so, with apprehension. Afterward Captain Truman told his men to get their four French 75s out of there, as fast as they could, for he knew the Germans nearby had zeroed in on practically everything in the Vosges, as the French had done too. The men of Battery D were a little on the slow side, as it was not easy to bring up the battery horses and hitch them to each 75 and get it out. Then a barrage of shells went shrieking its way over to the place whence the gas had come. "Run for the dugouts, fellows! They've got a bracket on us!" was the advice of the battery first sergeant. Captain Truman, who had to struggle out from under a wounded horse, was on his feet and began to tell "the boys," in stentorian tone and language, to get back up and take out the guns, which the men shamefacedly did for two of them, collecting the other two next day. According to the chaplain of the 129th Field Artillery Regiment, "he called them every name he could think of," which was a lot. Afterward Truman broke the ringleader, the first sergeant, and sent him to another battery. The battle became famous in the annals of the Sixtieth Field Artillery Brigade as the "Battle of Who Run."[18]

But this sort of experience was not at all what the division was to meet with later on, and constituted a useless series of exercises. They were not even field exercises, for in the Vosges there was no place for exercising anything more than a company, and to have done so would have attracted the attention of German gunners, who could not have allowed such an assemblage. Militarily the occupation of the Gerardmer sector offered considerable advantage to America's French ally, which was able to move its own troops out of that area and bring them in, tired as they were, as front-line or, more likely, reserve divisions in the hard-pressed line of the summer and autumn of 1918, when Britain and France had undergone a series of hammer blows in the offensives of General Erich Ludendorff, the skilled German field commander.

As the divisions came over in the late spring and summer of 1918 and swelled Pershing's AEF ranks from the bare 180,000 of late winter to a size that clearly was capable of standing on its own, the commander in chief insisted on his field generals receiving the responsibility of command that they desired. He organized corps commands and, late in August, asked for a sector for his First Army, newly organized, which he undertook to command himself rather than let someone else do it, despite his many other duties.

The sector assigned the AEF surrounded a salient that the Germans had occupied since 1914 in the vicinity of the town of St. Mihiel. The First Army gathered its divisions in front of the salient with the task of pushing it back.

St. Mihiel, it turned out, was not much of a battle. Pershing brought in 230,000 American troops against an opposing German force estimated at just 25,000. When the battle opened on September 12 the German defenders already were withdrawing. Pershing's First Army hurried their departure. Wags said afterward that it was an action in which the Americans relieved the Germans. The fighting, such as it was, occurred on the first day. The battle theoretically lasted until September 16, when the Americans could be sure the Germans were not going to counterattack.

Desiring to win at St. Mihiel, Pershing put in his best divisions. The Thirty-fifth was present but in reserve. It had nothing to do but stand ready. The men sensed their lack of participation and did not take the battle seriously. A corps inspector, to his horror, saw a sentry walking a post in the rain, carrying an umbrella. According to a witness, the sight threw the inspector into apoplexy and the soldier into the guardhouse.

So with the exception of the time spent in the Gerardmer sector, which the men would look back on as a vacation, and the previous small experiences, the summer passed uneventfully.

There followed a third failure in preparation, which succeeded the confusions that occurred, first, in the opening months of 1918, before crossing to France, when there should have been training in open warfare and liaison and instead was a march for a day, and, second, in the failure of the Thirty-fifth to learn much from a month with the British and a second month with the French in the Gerardmer sector.

The third failure was principally that of Pershing, in taking on the task of attacking the Germans in the Meuse-Argonne. That he did it was understandable, but it was not a wise decision. His ambition to see the AEF succeed drove him to expect too much of his troops. He had asked the Allied commander in chief, Marshal Ferdinand Foch, for a sector, and Foch gave him St. Mihiel, an enterprise well within the ability of the First Army to handle. Then late in August and early in September, Foch began to sense, and he was hearing this from the British Army's commander in France, Field Marshal Sir Douglas Haig, that the Allies might be able to win in 1918 rather than let the war go over into 1919. As a part of this larger strategy he went back to Pershing and asked the latter to make St. Mihiel a minor rather than a major operation. Pershing had had the idea of using the salient, once his troops occupied it, as a base from which to attack the German fortress, as it was described, of Metz. The approaches to the city had been fortified, and its capture would have been a coup for the AEF. Foch now did not desire that and instead wanted the Americans to move the bulk of their divisions at St. Mihiel fifty miles to the west to the Verdun sector and attack north and west in the Meuse-Argonne area. This was a challenge to the Americans, as Pershing at once realized. Impulsively he accepted it, trusting his newly organized staffs to carry it out.

The task of getting out of St. Mihiel, except for a few troops to hold the new line, and passing his divisions over to the Meuse-Argonne sector was huge. The commander in chief had to start the new attack exactly two weeks after his men had attacked at St. Mihiel. Understandably, he had assigned his most experienced troops to the St. Mihiel attack, as he did not want to fail there, and this left for the initial attack in the Meuse-Argonne mostly green troops such as the Thirty-fifth. It was a chance he had to take, he calculated. Then he had to get the troops into position to attack, something requiring moving a long distance cross-country. Gathering the troops in attack formation in the new sector, from the Argonne forest to the Meuse River, was an enormous operation, fortunately managed by the First Army assistant chief of operations, Colonel George C. Marshall. It was a Herculean job involving several routes over which Marshall had to allow for slow-moving animal transport as well as fast-moving camions, or trucks. For the animals there had to be stores of fodder along the way; for the trucks, gasoline. Unexpected confusions threatened to snarl the movement, and Colonel Marshall had to take them up and solve them, often more than one at a time.

A special awkwardness of the movement of troops was that it had to take place at night. The German enemy needed to believe that the AEF attack still was to go forward against Metz. Almost unbelievably, the German high command reinforced Metz and failed to grasp that the Meuse-Argonne was the danger point. But the troops involved needed the greatest possible discipline in this regard, which involved hiding in forested areas by day and keeping anything beyond normal traffic off the roads where investigating German airplanes would have spotted it. From the ground, on the American side, the night marches seemed near total confusion. The larger scene was wondrous, if it could have been observed. The Cleveland surgeon George W. Crile, a troubleshooter for the medical corps who was up and down the line, likened the preparation for the Meuse-Argonne to a huge, in daytime invisible, blanket of men and animals and machines and guns that their commanders were maneuvering up to the twenty-five-mile front, tugging and pulling at its corners, straightening it out, with each night of preparation.

It may be too much to blame Pershing for choosing the Meuse-Argonne, but it was all that his inexperienced troops could prepare for, and that they managed it as well as they did was nothing less than a miracle. Once their commander made his virtually snap decision, they sought, to their best, to follow through.

3

As the attack divisions grouped themselves, nine of them, along the line of attack from the Argonne to the Meuse, much obviously had been done. Unfortunately, and in particular for the Thirty-fifth Division, in line in the First Corps, with the Fifth and Third corps in, respectively, the middle and far right, many preparations had not been made. The Thirty-fifth was not in a position to do well when the whistles blew.

The artillery preparation for the attack was vastly impressive. The task of bringing up artillery—the light 75s as far forward as was safe, behind them the 155-mm guns, behind them the heavier artillery that was under corps and army control and was mostly for strategic use—had been accomplished.

The U.S. Navy, desiring to take part in land warfare, had sent up, on flat-cars, huge battleship rifles that threw twelve-inch shells that cast a greenish-white light and went over like freight trains, pulverizing anything that got in the way. The navy had sent up sailors in flat hats to serve the guns, and the hats were much in demand. Soldiers traded their overseas caps for the flat hats. The sailors were under command of a rear admiral with the appropriate name of C. P. Plunkitt.

Supplies for the divisions had been brought up, food and ammunition. There were first-aid stations at the immediate front, with triages farther back (the French word meant places for classifying wounds and directing the wounded farther back to special hospitals if necessary) and rail transport to hospitals deep enough into rear areas to allow staffs to treat patients without being fired upon by enemy long-range artillery.

But the men of the divisions, including those of the Thirty-fifth, were excessively tired. The Thirty fifth's infantry brigades, half of the division, had been moved by two hundred French trucks. The other half of the division walked, of course at night, and not in steady marches, although the movements by foot were so described. Because of the dark and crowded roads the pace had been hurry up and wait, to use the well-known army phrase. Sleep was difficult, all the way, because of the wetness in the woods and the cold—this was the north country, and autumn had set in. When the men arrived at last in the forests near the jump-off line they spent four days there under shell fire.

Most of the men had not taken a bath in a month, since they began to move toward St. Mihiel. At best they carried a single change of underwear, long since put to use. Their uniforms, unwashed, were the same summer ones they had started with. Winter clothing, requisitioned, had not arrived, and would not arrive until after the attack in the Meuse-Argonne.

The division's equipment was not in order, notably its signal equipment. According to army calculation, units as they advanced toward the enemy and presumably met sooner or later could choose between several modes for sending information to other front-line units and back to commanders in the battalions, regiments, and brigades and at division headquarters, with the last sending word to corps. Corps could summon assistance from its heavy artillery, or if necessary pull out a failing division—three were in line for each of the corps—and bring in a reserve division or, if the emergency were only partial, a regiment or brigade. All this depended on what messages went back from the front lines and how quickly the word traveled.

Given the importance of signal equipment, the Thirty-fifth was in very poor shape. The division's signal battalion did not get to France until June 11, after the division arrived. On the last of the month a representative of G-5, the training section of General Headquarters, reported that training in the battalion, and in several other divisions' signal battalions, was bad. In the Thirty-fifth, "due to orders for changes of location the equipment is kept boxed and no schedule is possible. The battalion has received no systematic training for its duties since its arrival in France." The division then was moving to the French sector, and French engineers operated the sector signal lines, with American signalmen assisting. The G-5 officer wrote that this method of preparing a battalion was "unsatisfactory and dangerous," which was no exaggeration.[19]

The division's two signal officers were incompetent. Lieutenant Colonel George A. Wieczorek was Regular Army, but before the war had been in coast artillery, a branch for which World War I had no duties, so its officers went overseas serving in other branches. Admittedly Wieczorek had gone to signal school. He was relieved before the offensive opened on the twenty-sixth. His replacement, Lieutenant Colonel Hans O. Olson, another Regular but an infantry officer, arrived on September 24. Wieczorek remained in charge until gassed on the first day. Olson tried hard, but his experience was slight. The division commander later pointed out that for three years preceding the declaration of war in 1917 he had been executive officer of the military prison at Fort Leavenworth, which "had not especially suited him for the work in hand."[20]

Telephones were the principal method of communication employed in 1918 by the signal officers, who sent out men to run lines and keep them in order—for the lines usually were laid on the ground where they were run over by trucks and torn up by artillery pieces and caissons, not to mention the havoc caused by enemy shells. Most of the wire available to American divisions was not insulated, wrapped with cotton rather than rubber. The Thirty-fifth found itself equipped with many miles—the new signal officer, Olson, turned in seventy to salvage after the division came out of the line—of the French wire known as "outpost wire twisted pair." The first rain, or even dampness, broke the circuits, ending all hope for messages. The Thirty-fifth did not have enough good wire; on the first day of the advance the regiments moved up an average of five kilometers, and some units had only two or so kilometers of wire. Then there was another problem with the wire, even that which was usable; it came wrapped on spools weighing 250 pounds, requiring carts. The signal officer of the 137th Infantry took the wire off the spools and rewrapped it on spools used for barbed wire.

Brigadier General Dennis E. Nolan, a G-2 (intelligence) officer at General Headquarters, served briefly as an infantry brigade commander with the Twenty-eighth Division to the left of the Thirty-fifth and observed his signal officer picking up and using German wire.[21] The Thirty-fifth did not do that.

Another form of communication, wireless, was possible, but the Thirty-fifth's regiments did not give their sets attention. One of the regiments could not use its set because it left all its signal equipment behind. The 137th Regiment discovered in the field that the amplifier of its set was broken and the batteries defective: Colonel Wieczorek did not pay attention to such matters. In addition, and it happened on the twenty-fifth of September, the day before Wieczorek was gassed and Olson took over, the wireless operator at division headquarters was unable to send messages to First Corps because no one could find the codebook with the corps call number. The next day, with the number secured, someone sent a message to corps in the clear, for which the corps chief of staff, Brigadier General Malin Craig, excoriated the Thirty-fifth.[22] An after-action report on the Thirty-fifth by the chief of staff of the First Army, Brigadier General Hugh A. Drum, apparently for this delinquency alone, criticized Wieczorek by name for incompetence.

Wieczorek took such a small part in the Thirty-fifth's operations that one of the infantry colonels afterward could not remember whether he had a wireless set. Nor could the chief of staff of the division, Colonel Hamilton S. Hawkins, although General Craig had received the offending message.[23]

To show their positions in the line, regiments and battalions could have put out panels that could have been read by planes of the French aero squadron assigned to the Thirty-fifth. There appear to have been only two sets of regimental panels, and they went to the two attack regiments, which took them from the support regiments. Some of the lower units could not find their panels, having either lost them or torn them up to use as rags. In which case, if they had wished to do so, they could have used—as some units did—underwear. After the Thirty-fifth was pulled out of the line there was much talk of inability to obtain information from the planes allotted to the division; tiring of it, the head of the AEF's air service, Major General Mason Patrick, compiled a detailed memorandum showing the division's inability with signals. Among his points was a comment about division headquarters, where soldiers allotted for the purpose always went out immediately and picked up messages from the planes that swooped down to drop them. On September 25 a flier dropped a message from one of the front-line units showing its position, read from panels, but when the message got inside no one could decode it. The division possessed the proper codebook, clef 326, but it could not find the portion of the code applicable to the division sector. Another copy was procured, but not until almost midday on September 26. As Patrick wrote, "The attack meanwhile had been launched at daylight of September 26 and reports received before the code arrived could not be read."[24]

A last resort for communication could have been Very pistols and rockets, and here there was a fiasco. Pistols were issued for signaling, then ammunition, and it was found that the latter was for pistols of another bore. A few hours before the battle a detailed list of signals was issued as an appendix to the battle orders, giving readings for specific rockets and flares. Six white balls of light in a rocket called for a barrage, one white and one green meant something, and two reds and a blue another, and so on. The materials were passed out, and it was discovered that all the rockets were "yellow smoke." No code on the list called for yellow smoke. As a critical account of the division published the year after the war concluded, "The signalers could only fire that one sign and it did not mean anything."[25]

One failure of the division to prepare for battle became a subject of major inquiry after the war, and that was the absence in the front lines of rolling kitchens, carts containing kitchen equipment. These did not get up to the front for several days after the division went forward. Men had to live on emergency rations of hardtack and canned beef. After the war Governor Henry J. Allen of Kansas, who had been division YMCA officer and was furious over the handling of the division that involved at least ten thousand Kansas troops, testified before the House Rules Committee and the Senate Committee on Military Affairs over what happened to the "bully beef" cans. Two pounds in size, they were too large for an individual; four soldiers were to share them. In practice the idea made no sense, for the man carrying the beef ate to satiety and then threw the can away—the front lines were littered, everyone admitted, with opened cans of spoiled beef. The division's commanding general by this time, Major General Peter E. Traub, remarked that the cans could have been divided with the portions for each man put in his mess kit, but that explanation made little sense—the food could not have been carried that way. As a result the men at the front rifled dead bodies, German and American, for whatever food their packs might contain. A favorite of the men was the large cookies carried by German soldiers, which sustained those fortunate enough to discover them.[26]

Anticipating a food shortage, Sergeant Triplet showed a considerable ingenuity, and described his procedure years later:

> I emptied my meat [messkit] can of toilet articles, went to the kitchen, and engaged First Cook Meagher in light conversation. While he was describing his current gripe in detail I snitched a couple of slices of French field bread and crumbled it into the meat can until it was well packed. Then I took the simmering pot of rendered bacon grease from the back of the range and poured the hot liquid fat to the brim over the bread. The resulting two pounds of congealed calories, cholesterol, and roughage wasn't a balanced diet but it should keep a man going a couple of days.

It proved too salty to eat, and Triplet threw it away.[27]

Details of lack of preparation lay on every hand. The corps orders for the attack arrived on September 24, and the regiments, the chief of staff, Colonel Hawkins, recalled, got their orders the day before the attack. He said they hardly had time to read them. The orders came too late for preparation of sufficient maps, and only battalion commanders had copies. They called their officers together and advised them to memorize what they could.[28]

Nor did the men have compasses by which to make their way over the tangles of barbed wire and shell holes and up-and-down geography of the Meuse country, where it was so easy to become lost. Only the platoon leaders had compasses.

As if all this was not enough, General Traub, who succeeded General Wright as division commander in mid-July, ensured trouble by making drastic changes of the division's senior commanders just before the battle opened. What Traub did was incompetence of a high order. Although one must say that just before the battle of Soissons on July 18, General Pershing did something similar when he sent two of his favorite commanders to the First and Second divisions. Soissons was a serious engagement in which the French commanded and the two American divisions formed the bulk of the attack. Charles P. Summerall went to the First and James G. Harbord to the Second. Both did poorly. Summerall had no control over his division, and his only response to heavy casualties was to order more attacks, resulting in the summary relief of his best infantry colonel, Conrad S. Babcock. In his short career as a division commander (after which he took over the Services of Supply, the AEF's rear areas), Harbord asked for his division's relief after a single day of casualties, and the French commander of the attack gave him his wish and replaced the big Second Division with a colonial division half its strength.[29]

Pershing did not seem to worry about changing commanders just before battle. In early September, the First Army, then under Pershing, inquired of Traub about his two infantry brigade commanders, and when Traub sent in adverse reports they were both relieved on September 21, five days before the opening of the Meuse-Argonne.

The brigadier of the Sixty-ninth Brigade, Nathaniel F. McClure, was Regular Army, and Traub later remarked that when he relieved McClure, a friend from his class at West Point thirty-four years before, he did it for the good of the service, because McClure could not put the leadership into his responsibilities that Traub required. McClure unceremoniously was sent to Blois, known as "Blooey" (hence perhaps the origin of *blooey*, meaning everything awry). It was a town where the AEF sent its officer misfits. McClure protested his relief and pointed out that he commanded the division for a month when it was in the French sector and there was no complaint from Traub until suddenly, just before the Meuse-Argonne, he was out. His was a saddening case, for he was reduced to colonel and sent home. His papers had gone to Harbord, as commander of Services of Supply, one of whose assistants sent them back with word that there was no place in the rear areas for an officer of McClure's rank.[30]

A more poignant relief, much more trouble for Traub, was the sending to Blois of the commander of the Seventieth Brigade, Charles I. Martin. When word spread that this had happened, officers gathered around him. The division armament officer, about to be commander of the 140th Regiment, Channing E. Delaplane, was in tears—a tough, and as it turned out reliable, man, he was not the tearful type. It was clear that Martin had a following, and his relief was no encouragement to troops about to go into battle.

It turned out that General Martin had been called to division headquarters in knowledge that he was to be reassigned but in ignorance that it was to Blois. The words of Traub to him were, "I suppose you know what it is all about?" Martin had no idea what it was all about and replied, "No, I do not." Traub said, "Well, up to the forepart of September I was required to give a report on my brigade commanders, and in your case I said that you had excellent tactical ability and the qualities of leadership, but that you lacked force, and as a result of that the order was issued."[31]

Traub testified to the First Corps inspector just after the division went out of the line that, as he put it, his brigadier lacked "the push, the vim, the energy, the enthusiasm, . . . [and] the spirit to carry out the work and orders to correct defects, and no urging could put those qualities into him." That array of necessary qualities, as the division commander retailed them, was sizable, and if true his statement was a considerable indictment. The division did need leadership, and Traub had a point. He explained to the inspector that he had been up against the lethargy of a National Guard division. His officers—Martin was a longtime figure in the Kansas Guard— were politically minded, he said, and pointed out that Henry Allen, his YMCA man, was running for the statehouse in Topeka and Martin was slated to follow him as governor. "My standard of discipline and efficiency," Traub told the inspector, "has never been attained to in this division. In spite of every effort I have made by orders, instructions and force of example, I have been unable to obtain this standard." He blamed this on a National Guard division. "This is the course of a National Guard Regiment, namely, the method of selection of its officers." From such candidates, and he did not say this but inferred it, come state-appointed general officers such as Martin.[32]

The principal point that Martin made during the postwar hearings was that he had seen Traub altogether five times prior to his dismissal, each of them only for a few minutes, twice in the sector in which he, Martin, was in command, three times at division headquarters, "and I do not think that he or anyone else could formulate an opinion in that time which would offset the opinion of the division commander who had been with me for a year, and who had not made any adverse report on me." Martin was speaking of General Wright. To this Traub replied that "my great experience of 10 months as brigadier and 7 weeks' observation of him in sector" had made judgment possible, and that he, Traub, as a major general had "a great many means of finding out about an officer."[33]

Perhaps the best response to the dismissals of McClure and Martin was that of the division machine-gun officer who in an article in the *Infantry Journal* in 1933 concluded that the dismissal was not fair to either McClure or Martin and the substitution of new brigade commanders on the eve of battle not fair to the men they commanded.[34]

Traub had undertaken what he would have described as a housecleaning, and in addition to commanders of the brigades he relieved each of his four infantry regiment commanders. The colonel of the 137th, Louis M. Nuttman, took over the Sixty-ninth Brigade, and the regimental command went to Colonel Clad Hamilton. The 138th went to Harry Howland the day before the fight. The 139th colonel, Kirby Walker, took the Seventieth Brigade, and the regiment passed to a colonel not yet arrived, so the attack was under Lieutenant Colonel Carl L. Ristine. Command of the 140th passed from Pierce A. Murphy to Channing E. Delaplane. These changes occurred between September 21 and 25. It was said that one of the new infantry commanders, dealing with his sizable regiment, at full strength four thousand men, did not know his three battalion commanders by sight or name, and such might have been true for other regiments.

There had been other changes during the housecleaning. The division had a new chief of staff, Hawkins, who followed two immediate predecessors. Traub in the last weeks had four G-2s, division intelligence officers. In the artillery brigade General Berry, never known for his sensitivity to anyone or anything, relieved the commander of the 130th Field Artillery Regiment, Lieutenant Colonel James E. Wilson, who had a permanent commission in the coast artillery, because Berry said he wanted Wilson's mental condition investigated.[35] He removed Colonel Frank Rumbold from the 128th Field Artillery on September 24, two days before the battle; Rumbold's health was bad, but he had hung on grimly, hoping to command his regiment through the ensuing fight.

The command changes, whatever their justifications, took place far beyond any sensible date before the opening of what was to prove the U.S. Army's most costly, and largest, battle in its entire history, from Revolutionary times to the present writing.

Two

Thursday, September 26

The sector to which the Thirty-fifth had been assigned by the First Army, which is to say by General Pershing, who at that time was acting as army commander as well as commander in chief at Chaumont, is not difficult to describe and appears on a map as a sort of channel moving northward a few kilometers and then shifting toward the northwest. It began with a front of twenty-five-hundred meters and after the turn widened rapidly to from forty-five hundred to five thousand.

The right boundary of the Thirty-fifth kept straight north from the jump-off line to the village of Very and turned slightly to the west as the Thirty-fifth's sector widened. Along that boundary was the sector of the Ninety-first Division, a green outfit like the Thirty-fifth, which its division commander described as capable of advance only with his personal direction, and which managed somehow to stay in line until Pershing called a halt to the initial attack on October 1 and reorganized, whereupon four of the attacking divisions, the Thirty-fifth, Ninety-first, and to the latter's right respectively the Thirty-seventh and Seventy-ninth divisions, could be gotten out. All green, all had failed—not much of a score from a total of nine attacking divisions. In the opinion of the First Corps and the First Army, the Thirty-fifth failed more than the other delinquents.[1]

The left boundary of the Thirty-fifth's sector ran along the Aire River, which in that portion of its winding course ran approximately north-south. The river made a marked bend to the west in the vicinity of the town of Grandpré and then wandered to the northwest, but the Thirty-fifth never got that far. At the beginning of the action most of the riverbed lay within the sector of the Twenty-eighth Division to the left. The country to the west of the Aire, shared by the Twenty-eighth and its next-door neighbors the Seventy-seventh and Ninety-second divisions, comprised the Argonne forest, a near-trackless elevation that would cause great trouble, for it allowed emplacement of German artillery in pits that were difficult to destroy because the soil of the Argonne was neither sand nor clay but a kind of composite that stuck together beautifully, from the German point of view, so that any gun pit was almost equivalent to having a gun placed in a cement revetment. To the west of the Ninety-second Division, which was to put only a single regiment in the line and only two of its three battalions, lay the French Fourth Army.

Country throughout the divisional zone of action was rolling, with open areas comprising parts of the sector, interspersed with woods. It was, the men might have said, much like Missouri. Captain Truman of the 129th Field Artillery could have espied country similar to what he knew near the village of Grandview, a few miles south of Kansas City. As he could look from his farm near Grandview all the way to Lawrence, Kansas, so he might have surveyed the Thirty-fifth's sector of the Argonne—save that the weather on the morning of the attack was not as he would have remembered in the late days of September. It was foggy and a bit on the cold side, sign that winter was approaching in the Argonne. Northern France, as all tourists in that area know, is like all of northern Europe, much higher in latitude than the heartland of the United States, subject to early autumnal weather, with much fog and rain, at such times not the sunny climate of Missouri and Kansas.

I

The battle of the Meuse-Argonne opened with a huge artillery preparatory fire that often has been described, and it indeed was impressive. Batteries ranged forward into German-held areas and blew all possible targets to smithereens. There were 3,928 guns of all calibers, 96.8 guns per kilometer. The French furnished 49.5 percent of them and the Americans the rest. The guns were arrayed according to size, with the lights, the 75s, three-inch

French pieces manned mostly by American artillery brigades—one brigade to each division, two regiments of 75s in each brigade—supported by French batteries of lights brought up for the occasion. Behind them, and at the outset sometimes with them depending on space along the army line, which was not all that much, stood the 155s, again French in manufacture. The American 155s—the third regiment in each U.S. artillery brigade—were supported by French heavies. Behind this array stood the heaviest guns. The 75s, as mentioned, were three-inchers; the 155s, six-inchers; while the larger calibers ranged up to the railroad guns as large as twelve inches, the guns that erupted with the greenish-white smoke and were served by the flat-hat men and commanded by the admiral.

The preparatory fire opened in what General Pershing trusted would be, to the German defenders, a confusing way. Guns in the St. Mihiel sector opened, and so did those in the sector of the French Fourth Army to the far west. The purpose was to confuse the defenders as to where the attack was going to come, that is, between the Meuse and the Argonne. Until 2:30 the fire was noisier from the Meuse to the Moselle, the Metz sector. Use of the St. Mihiel guns was important because there was a considerable German inclination to believe the Americans might attack the fortress of Metz in the country of the Woeuvre River, and they had reinforced the fortress in anticipation; prior to St. Mihiel they had let its defenses lapse as they took troops to other sectors, filling gaps or threatened gaps during the spring and summer offensives.

Actually, Pershing's staff prior to St. Mihiel had opted to go north to Metz, the capture of which would have broken the double-tracked German railroad that supplied the front for much of the defenses opposite the Allies. There was concern among AEF headquarters and First Army staffs when just before St. Mihiel the Allied commander in chief, Marshal Ferdinand Foch, asked Pershing to make St. Mihiel a limited operation, take on the Meuse-Argonne country, and threaten Sedan. There may have been sentiment in Foch's request, which verged upon a demand, and Pershing could have sensed it, in that the French Army of another era, during the Franco-Prussian War of 1870–1871, surrendered to the Germans at Sedan. Surrounded and in an impossible tactical position, the army was taken, along with the emperor himself, Napoleon III. A thrust to Sedan was more to Foch's taste. In the event, in November 1918, Pershing discovered that his troops were not designated for Sedan, but those of the Fourth Army. Even then Sedan was not taken, only threatened, and fell to French occupation after the armistice.

During the bombardments left and right on the night of September 25–26 the German high command remained uncertain what the Allies, including their associate, the Americans (technically the United States was not allied with the British and the French and fought only, as President Wilson put it, as an associated power), were going to do. The divisions of Pershing had come into the line surreptitiously, moving at night and under cover during daytime, this in the huge moving-blanket-like tactic described by Colonel Crile. French troops had been in line, and when the Americans came in they carried the subterfuge almost to an extreme. Officers when reconnoitering wore French uniforms. Lieutenant Colonel George S. Patton, commanding the First Provisional Tank Regiment, two battalions of American-manned six-ton French Renaults and a battalion of French tanks, wandered around the front of the Thirty-fifth Division dressed in a French uniform—it is bizarre to think of the redoubtable Patton clad in a French coat and hat. In any event, German intelligence was in a quandary, unsure where an attack might come.

At last, later in the night of September 25–26, uncertainty vanished: the First Army's guns opened. Among the defending forces in front of the First Army—the German First Guards Division, a regiment of the Fifth Guards, and a battalion of the Fifty-second Division—there no longer was a scintilla of doubt. The attack was in the Meuse-Argonne.

With the flashes of red, and behind them the rest of the heavies, the real preparation began. It continued until 5:30, when the barrage opened. The barrage advanced at four hundred feet per minute, behind which came the infantry.

In the First Army's preliminary bombardment for the Meuse-Argonne there was no question that targets were hit and in many cases obliterated, but it is an interesting issue whether the firing was as effective as it could have been. To be sure, any responsibility in that regard had little or nothing to do with the failure of the Thirty-fifth in the battle that followed. Responsibility for the bombardment was that of Pershing and the First Army. It is worth pointing out, however, that one informed observer, Colonel Lesley J. McNair, promoted to brigadier general in the last days of World War I, believed the bombardment was of little positive effect and even possessed disadvantages. Colonel McNair was to have a distinguished career during World War II, rising to lieutenant general and heading the Army Ground Forces, in charge of training the millions of American troops that fought in that war. In World War I he served in G-3, the operations section, at General Headquarters.

Colonel McNair considered the First Army's preliminary bombardment entirely wrong. In an operations report he wrote that such firing served no purpose. If the enemy was informed as to the attack, as was the case at St. Mihiel and, he said, the Meuse-Argonne (this was not true, as the German commander, General Max von Gallwitz, years later attested), such a firing forced him to a well-known tactic employed by the French commander just before Soissons when he learned of a German offensive due to open on July 15 and pulled his forces back, leaving suicide units in the front and second lines. The Germans at St. Mihiel and the Meuse-Argonne, he believed, had done likewise. What he favored was to precede the infantry attack with a short, fifteen-minute, violent bombardment.[2]

In his desire for a short preparation fire, McNair had a point. He did not think firing by the map was worthwhile, and he may have been correct. He was right in saying that a short preparation would induce the enemy to reveal his artillery positions, allowing attackers to handle them with counter battery fire.

He missed one point regarding fire by light artillery such as 75s, which would have made the preparation much more impressive, if nothing else scaring the German defenders out of their wits. This involved a possibility of the 75s throwing over far more shells than they did. A First Corps lieutenant from the corps inspector was with General Berry of the Sixtieth Field Artillery, the brigade of the Thirty-fifth, and saw Berry's two regiments of 75s firing slowly, one or two shots per minute, when it had been proved that for short periods 75s could do much more, as many as thirty shells in the air in a minute. At that rate there was the danger that the guns would get hot and blow up, but in short bombardments they could maintain this much larger fire.

McNair did not say that the following barrage advancing at a rate of four hundred feet per minute proved too fast for the infantry, which soon lost any advantage of following closely and catching enemy troops stunned and unable to fight effectively, perhaps even in their dugouts waiting for the fire to stop—as happened during the final American attack that began on November 1.

Behind any artillery failures was lack of experience. By November 1 the fine art of handling artillery had become an American specialty, almost as good as, perhaps equal to, the artillery work of the German Army.

During the preliminary fire one fact was certain on the American side, and this was that the American infantry regiments preparing to attack could not rest, could not sleep, during the din that went on around them and especially over their heads. The troops waited while the sheets of fire, small and larger and as big as freight trains, flew over. The sleep problem, which had been difficult for the Thirty-fifth beginning early in September, when the division started its move to go into support at St. Mihiel, and was not assisted by four days in the forest prior to moving into attack position, was distinctly not assisted by all the gunfire—but sleep was momentarily forgotten in the excitement of the waiting and the booming guns.

In understanding what happened, it will be helpful to have a few words about what sort of armament the men of the Thirty-fifth Division took with them as they went into battle, and then some account of how they went "over the top." The last words one employs advisedly, for the infantry entered enemy territory by plunging down a high bluff. They did not move out of trenches, but simply went forward and down into open country.

In addition to rifles and submachine guns, the Thirty-fifth's men took with them a mixture of equipment that was not all their leaders hoped for. Like troops in most of the other attacking divisions, they did not take 75-mm guns into the front lines, even though General Pershing showed great interest in the possibility and instructed his inspectors to tell commanders to do this. Such guns, if they could have been gotten up, would have done much service. But at 3,500 pounds they were far too heavy, each requiring six horses. Bringing them up, even with the horses, would have been nearly impossible over the rugged terrain of the Meuse-Argonne. The horses, too, would be highly visible targets for enemy machine-gun and artillery fire. After the war a study of attempts to use 75s in the front lines showed 143 efforts of one sort or another, not a single one of which resulted in anything.

Nor did two of the Thirty-fifth's regiments take along Stokes mortars and 37-mm guns (one-pounders), both of British manufacture, which if they would have been brought into the line could have hurled destructive three-inch projectiles or shells into machine-gun nests. The mortars and one-pounders had to be wheeled up. The tables of organization for mortars stipulated carts, but only two per gun were available. A mortar weighed eighty pounds and its tripod the same. Five more carts were needed for ammunition. The only available carts were those for heavy machine guns, the French-made Hotchkisses, and those carts had been condemned and sent to salvage. General Traub would tell the Senate committee that when the battle opened he was negotiating with salvage to get them back for use with the mortars and one-pounders.[3] Without carts the guns had to be lugged, not an easy task, and it took time to get them up.

The 138th Regiment did take mortars and 37-mm guns along—two 37-mm guns to the leading battalion and one gun and mortars to the support battalion—but they did not use them. The 140th Regiment brought up mortars and 37-mm guns and used them to good effect, although the men had to lug the ammunition, and that limited the guns' use. A first lieutenant in the 140th's mortar platoon, John H. Pleasants, was expert in putting out German machine-gun nests. A Regular, Pleasants exposed himself to German fire with a sangfroid that astonished Sergeant Triplet; he explained to the sergeant and his men that only a Chinese crossbow could touch him—during suppression of the Boxer Rebellion in 1900 he had been hit by an arrow.

Most of the division's heavy machine guns were not with the attacking troops. The Thirty-fifth had three heavy machine-gun battalions, one for each infantry brigade and one under divisional control. All but a few companies were brought together to take part in the barrage, raining bullets on suspected German positions. In the aggregate of machine-gun fire, from ninety-six Hotchkisses, with 150 or more (mostly more) shots per minute per gun, the Germans might have imagined themselves being attacked by a swarm of bees, a fearful sound. After the barrage the guns were sent up to the front.[4]

Some of the units of the Thirty-fifth went into battle without grenades, but lack of those weapons was not of large importance. A battalion of the 138th Regiment jumped off without them. It turned out that the absence of grenades did not have any effect, for Colonel Delaplane of the 140th wrote afterward that there was little opportunity in the actions to use them or even to use rifle grenades with their larger carrying power. The enemy machine guns apparently were too far off, and the artillery certainly was.[5]

The experience of the men as the rolling barrage opened and they moved forward was of a battle of movement, not trench warfare. Although they encountered trenches and barbed wire, formidable obstacles, maybe even impossible in trench warfare, all these barriers to rapid movement had fallen into disuse over the years during which the Germans held the sector, from 1914 onward. Revetments were there too, but they were full of rotten logs. They concerned Patton's tank men, for a Renault could get stuck in such places, teetering uncertainly, its treads churning and probably falling off. For the infantrymen they were merely places to scramble over or, in the case of barbed-wire rolls, scramble through after scouts cut the wire with big shears or found paths at the ends of rolls.

The men did not jump out of trenches but had to scramble down a rather steep series of banks, virtually like going down hills. Most of them remembered how they had to dig their heels into the dirt to keep from tumbling, getting out of balance because of their packs or baskets of grenades, managing to get down this initial barrier of sixty or seventy feet. Thereupon they found themselves in mazes of brush and vegetation with open places and woods, through which they stumbled along paths taken by their scouts and leaders. The latter individuals carried compasses and had simply to go north, if paths allowed. Only battalion leaders possessed maps—not many, in relation to the number of men, for each battalion had three companies, and each company had four platoons led by lieutenants or sergeants (there were insufficient second lieutenants to go around) and totaled 175–250 men under captains or, frequently, first lieutenants.

As if further to confuse matters, and at the beginning the men disliked the prospect, although they later understood how fortunate it was, they advanced in a heavy fog. Everyone remembered the fog, so typical of the Meuse country in early autumn, for as they went down the steep embankments they plunged into it. They could not see beyond a few feet. This, to be sure, was one of the reasons units became mixed, which mixing later would be furthered by other factors. Groups of men might loom out of the fog. If a guide, whether a scout or an officer, made an error in reckoning, then groups would be lost. No one had counted on this. One of the men remembered that the fog was spread evenly, "More like a spread-out blanket of white down." Sergeant Triplet recalled the fog: "Of course they had guides at the head of the battalion but how they kept their direction on that maze of trails is beyond me. Landmarks were invisible. By sunup time the fog was an absolutely blank white." Lieutenant Bancon, flying over the sector, dropped a message at division headquarters at 8:15 a.m.: "Impossible find line. Our sector is a solid white snow bank of clouds." Milton B. Sweningsen wrote fifty years later, "Somehow our squad kept together (and it appears that because of the fog . . . this went on all across our line) because we did come out in some sort of a skirmish line." Sweningsen saw a kind of grandeur in the fog, for as he stood on a bluff in front of a French village the fog seemed to sparkle, "and that is why the scene was so wonderful, so inspiring, so unbelievable—and so threatening."[6] Mixed with the fog was the smoke from smoke shells, part of the rolling barrage, theoretically an excellent idea but in this instance adding to the confusion.

And so the division began to move forward, in the order planned hastily after corps orders came down. It was a poised moment as men snaked their way down bluffs and went off along paths and over detritus of years before when French troops had attacked Germans in the sector, to no avail. The French had lost thousands of men in the Meuse country, hundreds of thousands around the half-ruined town, Verdun, that lay outside the American sector, below the far right-hand corner of the First Army's sector line. Verdun was a reminder of war before it turned fluid in 1918, with open warfare now the great tactical fact, as the Thirty-fifth was discovering. This was at the moment not to the pleasure of the scrambling men, as the units moved forward uncertainly, trying to keep skirmish lines in the brush of once-cultivated fields and patches of woods amid fog and smoke.

2

When the corps orders came down to the division, it was decided to move in column by brigades, with the Sixty-ninth Brigade under Colonel Nuttman spread out along the entire twenty-five hundred meters of the division line, the 138th Regiment on the right, the 137th on the left. In reserve was the Seventieth Brigade under Colonel Walker, 140th Regiment on the right, 139th on the left. To recite the disposition is, admittedly, complicated, although the logic is apparent. The plan was that the support brigade, the Seventieth, would pass through the attack brigade, the Sixty-ninth, on alternate days—meaning the initial passage would be on Friday, September 27. Each regiment contained three battalions, at full strength eight hundred men. The plan of the division was for a regiment to divide itself by battalions, one for attack, a second for support, the third in reserve. Each battalion contained four companies, and they too were assigned.

In the fighting that followed, for the Thirty-fifth on the first day the initial engagement was the taking of Vauquois Hill, an enterprise no one looked forward to. The hill was the largest eminence on the eastern part of the sector, assigned to the 138th Regiment with the 140th in support. First Corps considered Vauquois the most difficult barrier to be taken by any of its divisions, and with reason. The hill ran east and west and was long, covering a mile, more than half of the Thirty-fifth's sector line, and high, with a strangely appearing break in the middle of its crest, caused by an explosion during fighting, when that part of the crest had been blown off. Reportedly 30,000 Frenchmen (the figure varied, and sometimes appeared as 40,000) had been wounded or died while storming Vauquois, without result save their casualties. It was said that when French officers attached to the Thirty-fifth learned that the first objective was Vauquois they gathered in a small knot outside division headquarters, murmuring, one of them remarking, "Cré nom de Dieu." Said one, "That thrice-accursed hill again!" It was known as Le Mont des Morts, the hill of the dead. The Germans had revetted the trenches at its top in concrete. Inside, three hundred feet below the crest, were tunnels, connected to level galleries filled with high explosives. An entire infantry regiment could concentrate there and move about by narrow-gauge railroad.

What the attacking Americans did not know was that the garrison had been reduced to a fraction of what it once had been, a mere seventy-five men commanded by a nineteen-year-old lieutenant, Friedrich von Huellesheim. Because the Germans were uncertain that the Meuse area was in danger, the high command could not spare more. Most of the men had been called out of their tunnels and positions, back to the defensive line well above Vauquois, running from Charpentry to Epinonville. This was hardly a line, however, as on September 26 there was a gap across the Aire that the U.S. Twenty-eighth Division could have entered, if it had gotten up its sector quickly enough.

In the sector of the Thirty-fifth Division were units of two Guards divisions. At the beginning of the war each Guards division was first-class, but attrition had brought replacements of lower quality. Nor was unit strength what it once had been. At the beginning a Guards regiment had 3,000 men. Of the Guards regiments facing the Americans, one of them comprised 718 men, 132 noncommissioned officers, and 32 officers.

In 1927 the American magazine *Liberty* ran an article entitled "Five Red Days" and included a section from German sources in which Huellesheim, by then long out of the army, offered his diary. The document, which according to the magazine he sent home to his mother, did not have the ring of a diary and may have been invented for the occasion. For what the document was worth, it testified to the lieutenant's dilemma with his seventy-five men and six light machine guns. Part of it was the choice he was given, his division commander telling him to blow up the hill and retreat to the line of resistance, while his battalion commander was instructing him to "hold the hill to the last." As soon as the preparation fire of the Americans ended and his men came out of their defenses to see what they faced, they discovered the Americans around them on all sides, including the rear, where they were attempting to scale the hill to the tunnel entrance. No retreat was possible. This left Huellesheim with the second alternative, fighting to the last. The Americans were virtually invisible. It was possible to see a few, now and then, flitting through open places in the fog, but they disappeared before the defenders could sight a machine gun.

The lieutenant contemplated what to do, and gradually it became clear. Gathering all the men he could spare under an assistant he attempted a counterattack on the eastern portion of the hill. He ran through the underground tunnel to the west side where a reserve platoon was stationed. Along the way he found a few sappers who told him the platoon already had been used. The rest, as his diary described it, was simple. "I knew the game was up. Nothing could be saved but our honor. I dispatched two pigeons to carry our last message: 'Americans trying to ascend hill on all sides. Shall fight to the last. God save the King!' " With that, although the lieutenant did not say so in *Liberty*, he surrendered.[7] Vauquois fell in forty minutes.

Given the few resources for defense of Vauquois it was as well that there was little bloodshed. The entire 138th Regiment, nearly four thousand infantrymen, was facing Huellesheim, and behind it by a thousand meters was the 140th of similar strength. The Americans moved forward, the 138th leaving two companies from its rear battalions to mop up Vauquois and perform a similar service for the nearby Rossignol Woods.

Vauquois was just over the jump-off line, and three kilometers ahead lay the village of Cheppy, for which the 138th had to put up far more of a fight, requiring three hours and delaying the advance into afternoon. As General Traub, who had gone forward for the occasion, described the scene, the main German position was up a seventy-five-foot bluff a half kilometer south of the village, on the bank of Buanthe Creek, which was eight feet deep. Six machine guns were in pits at the top of the bluff. Two more were in a concrete emplacement halfway down. The right flank of the position—left to the American viewers coming up from Vauquois—was protected by a machine gun on the bank of the creek, and the other flank, to the east, by rolls of barbed wire. The position was supported by another machine-gun nest behind the defense line, in the village of Cheppy.[8]

The Germans waited until the American infantry was within two hundred yards before opening fire, and Traub thought this not a mark of unchivalrous behavior but due to poor visibility because of the fog. When fired upon, the men of the 138th dropped to the ground and dug in, replying with rifle fire. They attempted to turn both flanks of the position. On the west side they were driven back by machine-gun fire. On the east they found the barbed-wire entanglements. They discovered a road leading through the wire and attempted it, only to be forced back by machine-gun fire. Here the attacking First Battalion lost its commander, Major August R. Sauerwein, who was killed.

For a considerable while this was not a good situation. There was no signal connection with headquarters, either at the brigade or the division level. The signal platoon of headquarters company of the 138th managed to get a wireless set working in a shell hole and called repeatedly to tell of the plight of the regiment, but could get no answer. They obtained the time from the Eiffel Tower in Paris and heard other units' traffic but could not raise higher headquarters. There seemed no way to get support. The situation appeared serious. In hearings after the war, Governor Allen read a description by a Regular Army colonel—he held the name in confidence, but it was the colonel of the 138th, Howland—that sounded overdone, although the colonel could well have seen instances of what he described:

> Here, it seems to me, every officer and man did things during a three hours' heroic stand under constant high-explosive shelling and a murderous, direct machine-gun hailstorm from the front and both flanks, that is deserving of the highest recognition. It was a horrible scene, men handless, legless, armless, others perforated through and through, strewn over the field, in the road, in the ditches. And in spite of all this, the living held out gloriously for over three hours. . . . Oh, it was glorious, but so costly.[9]

An act of heroism occurred at this point, for it was necessary to find the location of the machine guns holding up the regiment and thereby the entire right flank of the division. Captain Alexander R. Skinker of H Company, who had three platoons with him, thought of using a Chauchat gun, the light machine gun of French manufacture that was regular issue in the Thirty-fifth (the Brownings, lights and heavies, were coming out of arsenals at home, and thousands were reaching the AEF, but General Pershing was wary of using them for fear of the Germans capturing one and copying it; the Seventy-ninth Division in the middle of the Meuse attack line had Brownings, but not the Thirty-fifth). The captain considered sending a gunner, but that required sending an assistant as well to carry the long clip and feed it into the gun. Skinker knew the gun and understood that if either the gunner or the assistant was cut down he himself could take their places. What happened was that he called a gunner and assistant and the three men went forward, heading straight for Cheppy with the bluff and its machine guns before them. First the carrier was shot dead, and Skinker took the clip and went ahead, feeding the rifle. Skinker fell next. Then the gunner. Scion of a wealthy family in St. Louis, the captain received the Congressional Medal of Honor posthumously. The Missouri Historical Society in St. Louis is located today on South Skinker Boulevard—and it would be interesting to know how many people understand the naming of that busy street.

The defense of Cheppy was broken by tanks. To the beleaguered men of the 138th they might have seemed like the U.S. cavalry of the West coming to the defense of settlers surrounded on all sides. Eight tanks suddenly appeared on the left. They maneuvered perfectly, in formation, and must have appeared to the German defenders as formidable, which they momentarily were. They swung out of column, turned into line, took position ten paces apart, with the infantrymen in the vicinity formed in squads behind. While the infantry fired on suspect places in the brush and woods on the bluff, the tanks pounded the machine-gun nests and pillbox, cutting guns and gunners to pieces. It all took minutes, eliminating an enemy that had delayed the advance until noon. The machine gun in Cheppy, behind the bluff, tried to stop the men of the 138th as they surged forward. Four tanks went in and cleaned the nest.

In the action before Cheppy there was a notable incident involving the First Provisional Tank Regiment's commander, Colonel Patton, which ended his part in the battle of the Meuse-Argonne. It did give him the action he so much desired. He had followed his tanks into battle, and like Traub with the 138th opted to observe their work. He could not do much more, other than watch. The tanks took two-man crews, with no place for an observer. He could not communicate with his tankers; there was no means, short of tankers putting their heads out of the hatches—no wireless, none of the gadgetry of later wars. Patton kept a diary, and after the action wrote of his experience. "Started forward at 6 a.m. H plus ½ hour. Heavy fog." He found men coming back, lost without compasses or maps, and took them with him. He and his group encountered heavy fire from the machine guns before Cheppy. The colonel managed to get to a railroad cut and sent a pigeon message, which probably did not get through; in the first day of the Meuse-Argonne the noise and fog and smoke confused pigeons, interfering with their homing instincts. At that juncture men from the Thirty-fifth Division came running back, and Patton and his men moved back two hundred meters. He believed he was being shelled by German artillery, although there is no evidence of shelling when the 138th was before Cheppy, only machine-gun fire. He might have heard fire from the barrage, which long since had passed beyond the infantrymen who were not moving at four hundred feet per minute. Many men were hit around him, "Lots of Dough Boys hit." He sought to make an "inft charge" with his men and "got shot." He and the other wounded lay in shell holes for an hour. He could hear the Germans talking, he wrote. "Went to hospital and was operated on by Dr. Elliot of N.Y." He had suffered several machine-gun wounds. The colonel thereafter believed he had gotten the tanks forward that saved the attackers at Cheppy and wrote that "we broke the Prussian guard with the tanks."[10]

At Cheppy the colonel of the 138th, Howland, was wounded in the hand and sent back to a hospital, and command devolved upon the regiment's lieutenant colonel, James S. Parker, under whom the men advanced to the next village, Very. Here the regiment did encounter German artillery, for the Ninety-first Division on the right had not been able to move rapidly through the Bois de Cheppy in its sector. This permitted the Germans to keep their artillery positions in Very. The 138th took Very at 3:00 p.m. and an hour later was a kilometer north. There it halted for the night.

Behind the 138th was the 140th, commanded by Lieutenant Colonel Delaplane. During the first day it saw no action and had not a single casualty. The men were busy, if only in walking the five kilometers from the jump-off. They had beaten clumps of brush, thrown grenades into dugouts, and otherwise, as one of the historians of the Thirty-fifth wrote, engaged in "making the neighborhood safe for democracy."[11] The 140th dug in for the night, as did the attack regiment.

For the 140th Regiment the first night of the Meuse-Argonne was bucolic, as Sergeant Triplet remembered it many years later. His platoon—there was no lieutenant and he commanded—had come up to a valley splotched with large shell holes, large enough to take a Sibley tent (the Civil War era tents he had known at Doniphan, circular affairs with holes in the tops for stove pipes, named after the Confederate general Henry H. Sibley). He and his men chose comfortable holes on the south side of the valley, ideal when a force was moving north, sheltering it from machine-gun and artillery fire except if enfiladed by fire coming in from the side, which was unlikely north of Very as the Ninety-first had caught up. Nearby was a battery of German heavy guns caught by American shell fire and destroyed. Some of the barracks for the gunners had not burned, and the sergeant sent men to search them and the vicinity for what they could find, hoping for what happened, discovery of field-gray blankets and loaves of bread, bushels of cabbages, six huge rabbits, and a cow. The latter two items were unusable and set free. Dinner that night was bread and cabbage, a welcome supplement to the unappetizing field rations the men carried. After dinner everyone went to sleep and Triplet remembered no unfriendly sound from either side until daylight.[12]

3

On the other portion of the division sector the 137th and 139th had been busy, but in ways different from those regiments on the right. The right regiments took two villages, Cheppy and Very, the latter almost straight north from the former. On the left were two more, Boureuilles and Varennes.

The villages at the left of the sector, unlike Cheppy on the right, offered no real problems to the attack regiment, the 137th. In front of Boureuilles the Germans had erected a small barricade across Route Nationale No. 46, the principal road in the Thirty-fifth's sector. The road initially lay on the west side of the Aire in the Twenty-eighth Division's sector and crossed at Varennes to run in that of the Thirty-fifth, all the way past Charpentry to Baulny, then on up close to Apremont and on to Fléville. In addition to the barricade there was a profusion of wire entanglements. The 137th had no trouble, perhaps because all this lay just over the jump-off line and the troops were fresh—that is, relatively so; if sleepless, they were fresher than they would be later on. Also the troops were largely protected by the fog and smoke.

Capturing Varennes amounted almost to an embarrassment for the infantry, as the tanks got up before the troops, and finding no Americans to hold the place went back down and came up again with the regiment. It could be said, therefore, that Patton's tanks, without their commander, who was pinned down before Cheppy, took one of the more important villages in the Thirty-fifth Division sector. Varennes was the locality where, in 1796, Louis XVI and his queen, Marie Antoinette, fleeing revolutionary France, seeking to escape into one of the German principalities, were captured by forces of the revolutionaries and sent back to Paris.

The taking of Varennes by the tanks amounted pretty much to the last tank action of moment during the Meuse-Argonne. Most of the tanks had been assigned to the Thirty-fifth Division, a few to the Twenty-eighth. The tank regiment lost forty-three tanks the first day, some to enemy action, others to mechanical failure. There was an extraordinary attrition rate for tanks in the field, and those that could move after a day or two were in need of full overhauls. The crews needed rest because of the heat and the rocking back and forth, with no provision for being strapped in or for padding in the spots where crewmen could strike their heads or be otherwise disabled. Tankmen were physically ill after any action of consequence; if the tanks were not disabled, the men were. Attrition in the tank regiment was no evidence of improper tactics with its tanks, however. In the attack on Amiens of August 8, 1918, the British used four hundred tanks, and of that number six were functioning on August 12.

More important in the left sector than capture of the villages were two great barriers in the Route Nationale that caused untold trouble for the Thirty-fifth Division as it attempted to send up its motorized and horse-drawn units. Two craters lay above Boureuilles on the way to Varennes. Making the first passable, not to mention the second, required far more time than it should have.

In the case of the first, there was little excuse for the failure of the Thirty-fifth and Twenty-eighth divisions to prepare for trouble. Both planned to use this road. The crater had been in the road since 1916, when the French feared the Germans were going to come down the road and took this method of slowing them. French engineers loaded a culvert, which extended under a thirty- or forty-foot embankment, with heavy explosives, creating a crater that was forty feet deep and ninety wide.

Failure to ask the French about the crater produced a fiasco. After the war an American engineer wrote in fury about the failure to find out the problem and prepare for it. He wrote of how his company made camp in Neuvilly, below the division jump-off line. There the men received so-called engineering equipment, which amounted to picks and shovels. When the infantry moved out, the engineer company started walking in the general direction of the front. They were two miles behind the infantry, and as they approached the fighting zone they could not calculate what was going on except "a jumble of cracking rifles, loud reports of firing cannon and explosions of incoming shells. The horizon consisted of a series of smoky masses caused from the burning of ammunition dumps by the retreating enemy." The air service, he wrote, was doing well. No German balloons were visible, save a few well down. Only one stayed in the air for a very short time.[13]

The engineer company had walked a kilometer or two when a great yawning gap appeared in the road in front, and trouble at once arose. Engineer officers had to decide whether to construct a bridge or a shoo-fly—that is, a detour—and chose the detour. As the men watched, more engineers came up, all with picks and shovels. In a fifteen-acre plot there soon were fifteen hundred men. Excavating began. A thousand feet of two-way-traffic road were to be constructed over a marshy, soft draw in the course of which there was to be an eight-foot wooden bridge. The road was to be of Telford base with a wearing surface of between six and eight inches. The detour needed at least a thousand cubic meters of Telford stone, but there was no stone. At Neuvilly a dump was full of Telford stone. But by this time traffic had backed up on the Route Nationale, and the first Mack truck full of stone was a mile behind in the jam.

The crater tied up traffic for twenty-four hours. About this time the First Army inspector, Colonel J. A. Baer, found the Thirty-fifth's chief of staff, Hawkins, at division headquarters. He was preparing to go to the crater and straighten out the jam. Baer advised him to send the traffic into small roads through woods, which he did. A single line of traffic was able to pass after a day, and in two days a double line.

According to the disgusted member of the engineer company, the second barrier, one mile ahead, another crater, had an additional problem. Fields on each side had been mined. A six-inch gun had been pulled on top of a mine and blew up, killing and wounding several men. Another shoo-fly was begun, but because of the impossibility of getting stone up from Neuvilly it was decided to build a plank road in place of the Telford. This took an entire day.

> By this means a two-way road was completed . . . and it was relief, the most appreciated relief, we had ever received when we saw the traffic congealed unravel, the great streams of cannon, ammunition, rations and everything war-going or war-making was pushed with the utmost rapidity to the front.[14]

The cost of these holdups from the two craters was very high. For one thing, the Thirty-fifth's artillery had trouble getting around the first crater, then the second, and the 75s, used by two of the three artillery regiments, had short ranges, eight thousand meters, and were dramatically needed as the infantry went beyond Very and Varennes up toward Charpentry and Baulny. For another, ambulances and other vehicles carrying wounded, many of them with men who had been in fields until picked up and moved to the edge of the road, then had to wait on the road. Judgment about the first crater should have been made well in advance of the attack. The first vehicles allowed on the road should have been the Mack trucks filled at Neuvilly. The second crater could have been discovered as soon as the German defenders blew it and the order for Macks doubled.

The craters were bad enough, but another factor entered. This was the inability of the attack regiment, the 137th, to handle German resistance above Varennes, which stopped the regiment four hundred meters north of the village. Immediately north and on the east side of the Aire was a horseshoe-shaped hill, wooded and rising abruptly fifty meters. The hill was studded with enemy machine-gun nests and artillery. The 137th located several of the nests and enemy artillery positions on this horseshoe north of Varennes and requested artillery fire on them, but by this time General Berry's barrage had ceased. The 75s were not merely out of range of the front line but, on the way forward, had been stopped in front of the first crater or, in attempting side roads through the woods, had sunk up to their axles in mud or wetland. Time was passing. Machine-gun nests were increasing. When the fog lifted around 10:00 a.m. hostile artillery to the north, especially across the Aire in the hills around Châtel-Chéhéry, commenced firing. Enemy batteries had zeroed in on all the places where troops could hide, such as woods. Fire into woods was doubly dangerous to troops because of falling branches and tree trunks. As for open areas, gunners on the heights could see American units standing around in them.

The 137th above Varennes was in place by battalions, the First on the road to the north, the Second on Hill 201 to the right, and the Third in reserve. A valley ran sideways toward Charpentry, and German machine gunners had only to point their weapons down the valley to hit anything that moved. The same thing held for the men above Varennes in front of the open mouth of the horseshoe. Men were in shell holes. The regimental commander, Colonel Hamilton, collapsed from exhaustion, and one of his men saw him in a shell hole, arms and legs stretched out, eyes closed. Spoken to, he would open his eyes and say whatever seemed to be needed.

At this juncture, with the 139th Regiment behind the 137th (it was in an orchard east of Varennes), the colonel of the 139th, Ristine, made a decision that later came in for criticism. At 2:00 p.m. he went up to the 137th and asked Hamilton what the trouble was, and received an answer that it would be suicidal to try to move forward.[15] As Ristine told the corps inspector after the division came out of the line, men of the 137th were filtering back through his lines, which was not a good sign. There was no artillery support from the Sixtieth Field Artillery Brigade, with the 75s on the road or caught in the traffic jam. Ristine did not know that, only that nothing friendly was coming over. German artillery fire, active since the fog lifted, was catching his troops, and it was a question of how long their morale would last, waiting for the 137th to move. He sent back runners to his brigade commander, Walker, asking permission to leapfrog the 137th, but received no answer. He believed he had a decision to make, and he made it. He took his advance skirmish line and scouts forward and left the regiment's two battalions (the third had been detached) with Major William D. Stepp, telling Stepp to bring them up. The skirmish line and scouts under Ristine's direction went around the top of the horseshoe, threatening to outflank the German machine guns and artillery, and the enemy force in front of the 137th gave up and moved back. During this time Major Stepp was not following, and the colonel returned to the orchard and found that Stepp had been killed. Unwittingly he had gotten into the path of a machine gun, stood up, and looked around as if he were at Santiago in 1898, and the gun cut him down.[16] Ristine led the two battalions forward.

For all this Ristine received criticism. His brigade commander, Walker, did not admire what he did; he was disgruntled about it. When the corps inspector asked Walker about the shift of regiments, the colonel said he was uneasy, for it put one of his regiments in attack with the other, the 140th to the right, in reserve. But surely Walker could have managed an attack by one of his two regiments, which would have called only for half his force in action when, on the second day, according to the division plan, he would have had both regiments on the front line.

Hawkins also was critical. When the inspector asked him about the passing of the 139th through the 137th he said the trouble was "the zealousness and inexperience of the regimental commander of one of the regiments of the second line."[17]

Walker and Hawkins were Regulars, and perhaps their criticism came from that fact, for Ristine was a Guard officer. He was temporarily in command of the 139th, for corps had assigned a Regular colonel to the regiment, but the colonel did not reach the regiment until Saturday, September 28. Feeling between Regulars and Guard officers was palpable. It was in evidence when after the action the corps inspector, a Regular, came up and was eager to point out in his voluminous report, submitted in mid-October, that the Thirty-fifth was a Guard division and subject to all the indiscipline of such divisions, which he blamed on Guard officers. When the chief of staff of the

First Army, Drum, sent a letter to Traub on October 26 harshly criticizing the division—quoting verbatim the corps inspector's seventeen points of conclusion, including a swipe at the division because it was a Guard unit—it was clear that the prewar Regular feeling against Guard units had not diminished.

But even a Guard officer, Major John H. O'Connor, who commanded one of the battalions of the 137th, attacked Ristine, accusing him of causing the breakup of the 137th Regiment. O'Connor spared nothing in his indictment, admittedly contained in a private letter, some years after the war, to the American Battle Monuments Commission.[18] In the 1920s the army established the commission to bring together the most exact accounts possible of the AEF's actions, drawing from division and other records that by that time had been gathered in Washington, and supplementing this information with memories of participants. General Pershing, whose term as chief of staff ended in 1924, was head of the commission. Some of the army's best officers took part, including Major Dwight D. Eisenhower, who went to France and helped write an official guide to the battlefields. Monuments were being erected by states, and the commission desired the legends thereon to be correct.

A staff officer of the commission in Washington solicited O'Connor, and he seized upon the opportunity. He was back in Kansas and active there as a Guard colonel and responded with vehemence concerning what his fellow Guard lieutenant colonel, Ristine, had done. O'Connor went after Ristine, saying he was an "inexcusable bonehead," that the leapfrogging was a "colossal tactical blunder," and that his own regiment, the 137th, was only trying to do its job when faced with the German machine guns and artillery to the north of Varennes, and Ristine interfered.

Still, there was a great deal to say for Ristine's decision. Certainly the 137th's breakup does not appear to have been Ristine's fault. From the outset the 137th was a command disaster. By early afternoon of the first day Hamilton (a Guard officer) had lost control. Signs of a breakup appeared when men from the 137th filtered back through Ristine's regiment. When the 139th went ahead, some men of the 137th found themselves surrounded and either went back or joined units of the 139th—Ristine, to be sure, gathered every 137th man he could find. The breakup came the next day, September 27, when there were two division attacks, morning and night, and the night attack units got lost, separated. During the night attack that second day O'Connor's battalion went far ahead and got out of touch with the two other regimental battalions. By this time there was no command structure. Hamilton, not physically able to handle the command, went to pieces above Varennes. The regiment's lieutenant colonel had been wounded, and command passed to O'Connor, who could not exercise it because he could not find the other battalions. Traub sent Hawkins up to take over the regiment, only to discover—this on September 28—that Hamilton felt better and was back in command (of a fraction of his regiment). On the twenty-ninth Hamilton had another relapse and finally left, with O'Connor again holding the bag until, that morning, the Regular colonel, who had wandered around, found the reserve battalion. Meanwhile, O'Connor had dropped out for a short time and lost his own battalion.

The result of Ristine's action was undeniably positive: on the afternoon of the first day, September 26, he gained control of the field, the Germans above Varennes retreated precipitously, and the entire line of the left side of the division sector moved up. When a halt was called for the night, by which time resistance again had stiffened, the 139th was across the Route Nationale one and a half kilometers northwest of Varennes, on the corps line for the first day. The War College study of the Thirty-fifth stated unequivocally that if Ristine had not leapfrogged his command, the division would not have reached the corps line.

Ristine's action came after he had tried to reach his brigade commander and could not. He had sent several runners back to find Walker and ask permission to go ahead, and there was no response. He did not try to reach division headquarters, which would have been improper anyway, out of channels, but it would not have done any good if a runner had gotten through the long distance to Mamelon Blanc, an eminence near the Côtes de Forimont, where division headquarters had been since the jump-off, well behind the starting line. Traub was up at Cheppy observing the 138th. Hawkins had gone off to unwind the traffic jam before the first of the two craters between Boureuilles and Varennes. Moreover, division headquarters knew nothing of what was going on. It had no connection with the actions right and left. A wounded officer from the 137th stumbled into division headquarters and found only the G-3 (operations) officer, Lieutenant Colonel Walter V. Gallagher. When he told the colonel and Captain Fullerton that Cheppy and Varennes had fallen, it was the first information they had. He desired to return to the 137th and asked where regimental headquarters was. "I wish I knew," Gallagher said, "and I wish I knew even where the brigade headquarters are." [19]

Behind the lack of liaison, regiments to brigades to division, were serious divisional errors. The plan of attack arranged for regiments in attack and support to be no more than two thousand meters apart. Colonel McNair in his after-action report on the Thirty-fifth thought that distance foolish; they were too close. It exposed the men to artillery fire. The G-2 (intelligence) officer of General Headquarters, Brigadier General Nolan, agreed. Like Mc-Nair, he was with the Thirty-fifth on the first day.

The attack plan invited a liaison problem. The trouble was arrangement in column of the brigades. Buanthe Creek went up the middle of the sector, northward, emptying into the Aire at Baulny, and was deep and almost dictated that brigades go in side by side. At Very and Varennes the sector commenced to widen, and the increasing distance from one end of the line to the other made communication ever more doubtful, the line doubling, increasing from twenty-five hundred meters to forty-five hundred or five thousand. Already overburdened, runners could not handle those distances.

Three

Friday–Saturday, September 27–28

In the two days after the attack the Thirty-fifth began to come apart, although its unraveling was not apparent to the division's brave men. The story is a subtle one, in which an error in judgment at army headquarters and a refusal to calculate its possibilities at corps and division headquarters led to increasing problems in the field. No single error, but an accumulation, lay behind all this. Perhaps the basic problem was the division's unreadiness after its indifferent training in the United States. It had no experience in open warfare in France. This was exacerbated by errors at the division level before the battle, such as the inability of division headquarters to pay attention to apparently mundane problems like bad telephone wire, the French wire known as outpost twisted pair. General Traub engaged in his housecleaning, changing commanders within days of September 26 and the jump-off. Then the men went over the bluff into the fog and smoke, momentarily exhilarated, but ever so tired because of a month of movement from one encampment to another, most of them in the wet and damp forest, which provided one poor sleeping place after another: possessing this basic tiredness they began quickly to wear out. By the second day, exhilaration having passed, they were tiring rapidly, and the third day even more so. And this just at the time when they needed every ounce of energy to make up for the lack of training and experience that lay in the past and the command errors of more recent origin.

The accumulation began to show on September 27 and 28, and the result was immediately unpleasant. To units in the field it seemed only to be what Karl von Clausewitz referred to as the fog of battle, and by and large they took it in stride. It was much more than that, however, for it promised disaster.

I

There were two attacks by regiments of the Thirty-fifth on Friday, September 27, both ordered by General Pershing, the first a failure, the second a qualified success.

In the first attack a muddle developed over the attack time. The division chief of staff, Hawkins, who was forward, to the south of Cheppy, ignored a corps order for an attack at 5:30 a.m. and issued an order for an attack at 8:30 a.m. He knew the division had a large problem with getting up its artillery. The preceding morning, after the infantry moved out, the two light regiments of artillery soon found their guns out of range and took to the road, or at least what was available of it. They were stopped by the craters beyond Boureuilles on the Route Nationale and detoured to small side roads not really suitable for artillery. The going was doubly difficult because of the condition of the horses, virtually exhausted by bringing the guns up to the firing line to support the attack on September 26. The horses were poor, anyway, and word had it—denied by General Traub during the congressional hearings—that some of them were good for two hours and no more. The regiments did not bring over their horses from the United States, and the AEF had gone into the local market for horses. Veterinarians had instructions to buy anything that could stand. In the hearings it was said that they paid top dollar, $400, for disgraceful nags, some of them gassed and sent back from French regiments.[1] Somehow during that night of September 26–27 the men of the 128th and 129th, assisted by whatever horses survived the night, got guns forward.

From descriptions of getting the guns into range to support a preparation fire and rolling barrage on the morning of September 27, it appears that Hawkins had more appreciation of this problem, perhaps a good deal more, than did General Traub. Hawkins had seen the traffic jam on the Route Nationale. As for the horses, it is arguable that such details should concern a division commander who has to deal with larger problems. A counter is that larger problems usually are composites of small ones, and in this case the horse problem, brushed off by Traub during the postwar investigations, nearly in itself governed what was possible. The horses had to pull the guns through the side roads, sometimes hardly more than fire trails in the woods. It was the "for want of a nail" problem. Traub had a habit of ignoring matters that demanded the attention of someone, assuming, as he was fond of saying, that a commander not merely had subordinates but that they were doing their jobs.

When Traub learned that Hawkins had delayed execution of a corps order he countermanded Hawkins's order, moving the attack time back to what corps stated, 5:30. He was not about to violate an order through corps that came from General Pershing, the commander in chief. Shortly after 1:00 a.m. he sent the order: "The Thirty-fifth Division will attack the enemy at 5:30 a.m. this morning and advance to the combined army first phase [line] east of Fléville."

Traub's order showed no sensitivity to the tactical situation, the all-night work of the German opponents in bringing in reinforcements and getting the machine gunners into place, the difficulties of getting the 75s into position because of the roads and weakened horses, then the assignment of an impossible goal, Fléville, far up the Route Nationale, when the troops were only above Varennes. On the artillery issue the order by Hawkins for 8:30 offered specifics of support for the infantry. Traub's order dealt in generalities; it gave only instructions for artillery to assist by barrage after consultation, however that could be done.

Traub then realized that if his 5:30 attack order did not get through to the regiments and battalions, there could be a ragged attack. It would be worsened by his artillery firing into lines it was unsure of; the men would be caught in their own fire. He decided to go forward with the orders, and did so in the company of the division inspector, Captain Edward C. Sammons. The two came into Colonel Walker's command post south of Cheppy at some time after 4:00 a.m. The commander of the Seventieth Brigade was exhausted and hardly able to talk with the division commander, who asked if the brigade had received the 5:30 order. Hawkins meanwhile had confirmed the 8:30 order. Traub told Walker that 5:30 had to be the time: "It is General Pershing's order; it must be done." Walker and his staff explained to the divisional commander that time did not allow for getting word to the battalions. On the right of the sector the 140th would have to pass through the 138th. This change in attack regiments would not be necessary on the left, for Ristine's 139th (also in Walker's Seventieth Brigade) had made the passage through the 137th the day before. Traub made a compromise, that the artillery was to begin firing at 5:30 and the infantry advance at 6:30.

Orders had to get to the artillery at once, so that it could give the infantry a rolling barrage at 6:30—after preparation fire opened at 5:30. At this time Colonel Ristine was at Walker's post of command, and it fell to him to get the word to his own regiment. Major Norman B. Comfort went back inside the command post where the meeting had been held, a former German structure, to waken a runner who was the only person, other than Comfort, who knew the way to the artillery. He shook the man, to discover that an incoming shell had killed him—the walls of German huts and dugouts faced the wrong way, with their entrances open to enemy fire. Comfort mounted a horse and carried the word himself.

The next morning the advances in each half of the sector were failures. On the right the 140th Infantry passed through the 138th, part of the plans of both Hawkins and Traub, so as to bring both regiments of the Seventieth Brigade into the front line. There was virtually no artillery support. Many troops observed none, other than shells from what seemed a few guns and in fact were. The only artillery battalion in line, from the 129th Field Artillery Regiment, had to support both of the attacking regiments. The corps inspector afterward asked Colonel Delaplane how long his line was, and the answer was nine hundred yards, a half mile. If half of the barrage shells went in front of his line, that meant one- and one-half batteries out of the battalion's three, four guns to a battery, six guns total, firing ahead of an infantry line that stretched half a mile. Berry's usual allotment of shots was one or two a minute for a 75 gun, which at best allowed him twelve shots each minute to cover half a mile. First Army specified one battery covering every four hundred feet for a barrage. The barrage that morning had one battery covering eighteen hundred feet. It was ridiculous.

The barrage, if it went over as described above, could hardly have been worth the name, but it is possible that another factor made the infantrymen think they had no barrage. Karl Klemm, the colonel of the 129th Field Artillery, the only regiment that had batteries within range, told a Kansas City newspaper after the war that he learned of the need for a barrage at 3:00 a.m. on the twenty-seventh, but it took until 6:00 a.m. to get word to the batteries. The delay was caused not by a failure of telephone communication—the Sixtieth Field Artillery Brigade had good wire—but by a need to work out a perfect time schedule on the advance of range to keep the batteries firing together and make sure that none of the shells would fall short into the advancing troops. At last compiled, the schedule went to the batteries and fire started, Klemm said, at various periods ranging from 6:30 to 7:30.

For the infantry action of the morning of September 27 the colonel of the 140th, Delaplane, who like Ristine was a first-rate commander, cannily put only a single battalion on the front line, keeping his attack force thin, with two battalions in support. This was fortunate because the Germans, with their machine guns and artillery, were waiting for him. He had gone no more than half a mile, to the top of a crest and a little beyond, when his men met hailstorms of machine-gun bullets, were pounded by artillery, and had to call it quits, stop, and dig in. They were nearly boxed, with fire coming from the front, the right, and the left. The Ninety-first was absent on the right, exposing the regiment to the flank fire there. On the left beyond the Aire the Twenty-eighth Division had not yet come up.

On the left side of the division sector, Ristine's line ran into the same thing, although it was nearer the artillery pits high up in the ridges of the Argonne and, if anything, received more fire. Unlike the colonel of the 140th, Ristine put two battalions in the line, the First and Third, along with two companies of the Second. The Second's remaining companies were on liaison or in reserve. His men were grouped more thickly and took more casualties. At 6:30 a.m., his men poised, he waited for the barrage—and nothing came. He sent back word for the barrage and received no answer. At 9:00 a.m. he attacked without support. The left battalion went forward six hundred meters, a third of a mile, and with the aid of tanks the right battalion came abreast at noon.

During that morning and after the failure of the barrage the 129th Field Artillery did its best to assist the infantry regiments, but the latter failed to give the artillery enough information. Klemm said the situation was impossible. "We want a barrage at once," would be the request.

"Well, where are you?" he would inquire.

"Why, we're in such-and-such a place in a ravine," the infantry unit would say.

"Where are they coming from?"

"We don't know, they're coming over the top of the hill."

It was at noon that the First Corps gave special attention to the Thirty-fifth Division. General Craig was uncertain of the Thirty-fifth after the slow going of the morning offensive, and he was disgusted by the fact that division headquarters was not telling him much and, beyond that, when anyone tried to find Hawkins or Traub they were out somewhere—it had happened on the first day, and they were out again on the morning of the second. It is unclear if he knew of the muddle in orders over the attack that morning. He probably did. At noon on Friday the twenty-seventh, he sent a colonel from corps operations, Jens Bugge, to be acting chief of staff of the Thirty-fifth. He told Bugge, "Get up there as soon as you can and put some punch into it."[2]

Late that afternoon Traub at the Côtes de Forimont was chafing over the failure of the morning attack and planning another when he received a message that made things clear:

> 27 September, 4:30 p.m.
> From C in C.
> He expects the Thirty-fifth Division to move forward. He is not satisfied with the Division being stopped by machine gun nests here and there. He expects the Division to move forward now in accordance to orders.

Traub possessed uncertain connections with his infantry brigades and they with the regiments, and time was short—in northern France late in September darkness would be approaching by 6:00 p.m. He sent up an attack order for 5:30 p.m., which fortunately the commanders of the 140th and 139th regiments were able to handle.

By this hour the artillery situation was far better than in the morning. A battalion of the 129th Field Artillery Regiment had joined a battalion of the 128th at Hill 221. Two batteries of the 129th were in position at Cheppy. The 130th, the heavy regiment with 155s, was in position at Varennes—it had gotten up the Route Nationale, passing the craters above Boureuilles, churning up whatever roadway was left from one of France's once better highways. One battalion of the 128th and one battery of the 129th were not in place.[3]

Tanks still were available, although the Germans were bringing up anti-tank guns, seven-foot squirrel rifles with bores of an inch, three times those of Springfields and Lee-Enfields. On the first day none was in evidence; by the end of the second they were gathering.[4]

On the right side of the division sector the 140th attacked with a single battalion, Delaplane again showing caution. The attack battalion, the Second, advanced two hundred yards north of the Charpentry-Eclisfontaine road. It came up to three hundred yards northwest of Very. In the attack it took the enemy machine guns in front of it. The Germans had emplaced artillery pieces, in knowledge that if the Americans were successful the pieces would be lost, and so they were. During this evening attack the support battalion of the 140th, the First, passed through the left flank of the attacking Second Battalion, advancing a kilometer farther to the northwest. The two battalions were considerably mixed. The Third Battalion was in reserve.

The movement of the 140th's First Battalion up a kilometer to the left of the attack battalion constituted a very interesting development, and it is intriguing to speculate what might have happened if that battalion had kept on going. Sergeant Triplet, who was a member of the First Battalion, later thought that it might have been possible to keep on, through Montrebeau Woods, straight north to Exermont and farther, to the top of the hill named Montrefagne, and maybe even beyond that. It was clear, he wrote, that a breakthrough might have been made. His battalion was getting little opposition. There did not seem to be many German troops in the vicinity. All of which made sense in retrospect, for German lines were extended to the utmost. A gap had existed ahead of the Twenty-eighth Division to the left, which that division failed to fill. In the area of the Seventy-seventh Division to the left of the Twenty-eighth, the German defenders in the Argonne forest were at the outset very few, and Colonel McNair, who observed the Seventy-seventh on the first day and saw its men sauntering, as he put it, into the Argonne, greatly regretted what he guessed was their failure to seize an opportunity.[5]

When the First Battalion got ahead and to the left, a runner came up from the company to Triplet's platoon and told him to halt the men where they were. Perhaps it was an order from the regimental level. It could have been a battalion order, given by the First Battalion commander, Major Fred L. Lemmon, who momentarily was incapable of thinking straight; he had been shot in the chest by a bullet that fortunately did not penetrate his lung but broke several ribs. In any event, if it was a missed opportunity neither Delaplane nor Lemmon was at fault, for to seize it would have required support from brigade and division. The Thirty-fifth was too loose an organization to exploit such an opportunity. It is sad to think of the possibility.

On the division's left sector Ristine with the attack regiment, the 139th, did not have much time to prepare, receiving Traub's order at 5:00 p.m., giving a half hour, but because at that moment he was consulting his battalion commanders he was able to gather his men. The attack there went off at 5:30 p.m. Charpentry was taken at 6:00 p.m. The battalion of the 139th in front, the First, inclined to the left after leaving Charpentry and reached and went through Baulny. The Second Battalion, under Major James E.

Rieger, less two companies serving as liaison, arrived at Chaudron Farm at 7:00 p.m. and went on forward to the eastern edge of Montrebeau Woods, two-thirds of a mile ahead to the northwest, the high point of that evening's advance. The woods was a dense thicket of trees and underbrush that was to become better known the next day, the twenty-eighth.

Elsewhere the advance, which if measured by Major Rieger's battalion of the 139th was two and one-half kilometers—when added to the first day's five kilometers that made a total of seven and one-half kilometers, or five miles—was going well. At 10:00 p.m. a report came in from Rieger that the 140th Infantry's First Battalion was on his right, a kilometer to the rear. The Third Battalion of the 139th under Captain Henry F. Halverson—Ristine's men were all doing well—with three companies reached Montrebeau Woods. Losing touch with the Second Battalion, it fell back to the Baulny ridge. A mile or so below Baulny the First Battalion of the 139th seems to have crossed the Aire and occupied Montblainville.

It was not easy going that night, and much of the advance was in darkness. This raised a prospect, not realized at that time but taken advantage of weeks later on the nights of November 2 and 3 by the Second Division, one of the two point divisions of the attack on November 1 in the spectacular advance of the central corps, the Fifth. Coming up against machine-gun nests the Second formed itself into a huge, winding column and passed up and beyond the then German line. Enemy machine gunners could not see their targets in the darkness, and the same held for artillery units. At daybreak the Second Division surprised enemy troops in rear areas, bringing consternation to the German command.

Sergeant Triplet of the 140th, writing years later, remembered what might have happened when the Thirty-fifth Division made a virtual night attack at 5:30 p.m. on September 27:

> Yes, if I were a general I'd send my outfit in about 0300 through the black night and fog, have them move through the lines by platoon columns one to five miles, and then just dig in and wait for daylight. That would sure raise hell with a defensive system. When the main show started at sunup the Jerry reserves would be fighting forty-eight little wars on sixteen different fronts, his artillery would be driven from their guns by small-arms fire, and his outpost line would crumple like tissue paper.[6]

In a small sense this is what happened when Pershing's favorite tactic of attack, and his knowledge that in the opening day of the battle he had the

Germans off guard, and soon would have them reorganized, moved him to shove the Thirty-fifth.

The tactic worked best against enemy troops spread thinly, as was the case both on the night of September 27 and with the Second Division on November 2 and 3. One can only wish that the Thirty-fifth had been as well organized as the Second and could have gotten up into the German rear areas in full force, moving its artillery up there too. It might have obtained a breakthrough into the high country to the north, maybe even have gotten up—it would have taken a day or two—to the Meuse itself. According to the commander of A Company of the 137th, on the evening of September 27 his men got into a gap in the German line. First Lieutenant C. B. Allen, in charge of the company, kept up the advance after dark, toward the army objective, Fléville, believing the right flank companies of the 137th and 139th were still on the advance. Meeting no resistance, he made his way across a bridge below Charpentry that the Germans had overlooked with their mines and by 9:00 p.m. had penetrated four kilometers. He picked up a platoon of machine-gun men that had become separated from its main body and attached it to his command. He then began to realize that the right flank of the attack had received later orders to stop at the ridges somewhere to his right rear. Putting out a flank guard and front and rear patrols, he proceeded on up a road to the right until his company was almost directly in front of the main body of the 137th and 139th. Here, while drawn up to the side of the road, his rear guard became engaged with a few Germans, who wounded one of his men. The Germans were quickly dispersed, and the lieutenant drew the company, now quite large with the machine gunners, up to the side of a small hedge overlooking the road, where he stayed for a few minutes to "let the excitement quiet down and refrain from stirring up any further outbursts." His company was, he wrote, surrounded by the enemy, except for an opening that he had come upon earlier in the evening. At 10:00 p.m. he reversed the company and began a countermarch, working by compass, through the night, back to the main line, avoiding skirmishes. He wrote that he had formed the company so carefully, with scouts in all directions, that if necessary he could have put up stiff resistance to a large body of the enemy.[7]

The Thirty-fifth was not the Second. There could be no breakthrough with General Traub's lack of brigade and division command and with the 137th Regiment disintegrating.

2

On Saturday, September 28, the division extended its lines to the top of Montrebeau Woods. This was a thick tangle of trees and brush a square kilometer in size, and a Missouri farmer might have guessed it at six square forties, or 240 acres. The exertion of taking the woods was large, and the disorganization of the evening before increased noticeably.

Artillery positions were the same as the day before. During the night of September 27–28, Berry had been unable to move his guns forward because the late afternoon attack lasted until 11:00 p.m. He then received the attack order for the morning of the twenty-eighth and found that his 75s could cover the entire proposed advance from their positions. His only problem on the twenty-eighth was a message from Traub that complaints had come in of short firing. He investigated and believed at the time, and told Traub, that the shorts came from the French batteries attached to his brigade, which moved back from positions without informing him. He sent word that they should lengthen their range. When he asked Traub if any more reports of shorts had come in, the division commander said no. Berry of course did not help the situation much by telling the French to shoot farther, for he was asking them to continue firing by the map, without visible targets, so that their fire was of no immediate benefit to the men in the front-line infantry, who often were in need of fire on obstacles such as machine-gun posts just ahead of them. In investigating the short firing he later changed his mind about the source of the trouble, believing that the front-line men were confused as to where shells were coming from and likely the source was German flank fire.

On the morning of the twenty-eighth the disposition of the regiments was far from perfect but still possessed the outline of order. On the right of the line Delaplane had control of his regiment. The 138th Infantry under Lieutenant Colonel Parker lay to the right of Delaplane's 140th. On the latter's left the 139th together with remnants of the 137th was on the Baulny ridge. The two left regiments were now badly mixed. Both commanders, too, had changed. On the night of September 27–28, in the front line as usual, Ristine had taken a wrong turn and gotten lost, entering German territory to the west of Montrebeau Woods. He was to remain lost throughout Saturday, September 28, not turning up until early on the morning of the next day, when he wandered into the lines of the Twenty-eighth Division across the Aire to the west. His absence was a major loss, for his had been a real leadership. After he disappeared the regiment went ahead for a while without a leader. On Saturday the twenty-eighth it was without regimental organization. Ristine's adjutant had been killed, and the lieutenant whom the colonel had hoped would take the adjutant's place was wounded. The liaison officer, signal officer, regimental gas officer, and the three officers in charge of the Stokes mortars and one-pounders were all casualties, so no officer was left to establish a new command post. Major Rieger, ahead with the Second Battalion, did not know that Ristine was lost in the German lines. The Third Battalion was commanded by a lieutenant. The First Battalion was in command of a captain, and he had one officer per company left. As for the 137th, it similarly was in a leadership confusion.

At the same time, the German defenses were coming together. The First Guards Division was wearing out and would be withdrawn, its effectiveness down almost to nothing. The Fifth Guards was in better condition. It was reinforced on September 28 by the Fifty-second Division, a regiment of which may have entered the line the day before. Antitank guns were now at hand, which tended to cancel the advantage of tanks on the American side. The Germans were in control of the air and on the twenty-eighth sent over planes at will. The planes were nuisances to the infantry, as they flew up and down the lines machine-gunning. It was true that their bursts were far more frightening than damaging, as their fire was not very effective. Far more important was their uninterrupted spotting, at which they were skilled. Within minutes of their appearance enemy batteries far in the rear would open. Enfilading fire came from the direction of lagging AEF divisions on either side, the Ninety-first and the Twenty-eighth. High up around Châtel-Chéhéry nineteen batteries opened.

After the first day the weather turned rainy and cold. Private Sweningsen of the 137th remembered that the drizzle became a cold rain. It was difficult to ditch around his sleeping place because the ground was so hard. "The rainwater began to run down the hill into my diggings."[8]

Men were increasingly tired, having slept little since the night before the jump-off. The next two nights, with the exception of fortunate soldiers like Triplet, had been nearly sleepless.

The rolling kitchens were not up. The recourse was to discover stores of German rations or remove food from packs. Supplies of fresh vegetables and beef were being sent up, but they were useless because the men did not dare make fires to cook them, and there was no charcoal or canned heat.

The morning attack on the twenty-eighth opened raggedly on each side of the line. On the right, at 3:30 a.m., Delaplane received an order to take his regiment forward as soon as possible to protect the flank of troops on his left. The 139th and 137th on the left were to attack at 6:30. Delaplane had his men underway at 5:30. He barely got forward when by 8:00 a.m. he faced withering fire from machine guns and artillery and stopped and dug in. At 9:45 tanks came up and the 140th tried again. The advance was very slow. There did not seem to be much artillery support. One of the Thirty-fifth Division histories, that of Clair Kenamore, related, "It was the bloodiest hour the 140th Regiment had seen. The regiment advanced, but paid a heavier price than it ever had before. The tanks were not as effective as they had been."9 The antitank guns were in action, supported by light artillery pushed forward to fire point-blank and to be abandoned if necessary. In the early afternoon, 2:30, Captain Ralph E. Truman, intelligence officer of the 140th and first cousin of the captain of Battery D of the 129th Field Artillery, sent the following message:

> Regiment halted by terrific artillery shelling and concentrated machine-gun fire. See drawing showing approximately our front line. There may be a little change made during the night. We are flanked by artillery fire on every side but our rear. Our own artillery has given no support during the attack. Enemy planes were active during the day. One squadron of enemy planes over our position at 1 p.m. They turned their m.g.'s on the men, causing some losses. Fifteen planes in the party. Also one enemy plane flew low over our troops all during the forenoon directing the fire of the artillery. We have suffered heavy losses in killed and wounded. Men are still at dressing stations that were wounded yesterday. Numbers of men who are wounded have had no attention and are still lying on the ground where they fell. We are short of ammunition which is very badly needed in case of a counterattack by the enemy. The adjutant has been gassed and the C.O. has not been seen since the attack started. Runners unable to find any trace of him.10

By this time Delaplane had gotten separated and was on the Chaudron Farm road above Baulny, hemmed in with a company of the 129th Machine Gun Battalion and sixty struggling infantrymen who had lost touch with their units. At 6:45 p.m. he sent a runner to division headquarters with this news and rejoined. The well-run regiment had been on its own during his absence.

Captain Sammons, division inspector, and a fellow officer had come up to the front abut 4:00 p.m. and found the 140th on the right and two battalions of the 139th on the left, both running like clockwork.

On the twenty-eighth the 138th, which had gotten to the right rear of the 140th after the latter's morning attack, lined itself up with Delaplane's regiment, to help fill a huge hole in the line with the Ninety-first Division. An artillery officer in the area between division sectors wrote that the gap approached four kilometers, an invitation to enemy troops. According to reports, the left of his division had shifted toward the right and was almost totally unofficered. His battery was put on alert. "The mechanics were called up and instructed in the approved mode of wrecking the guns, should we be compelled to leave them. . . . Pull out the key, 'feed her a shell and pull the string.'" Most of the battery side arms had been lost in the move to the front, but the machine-gun squad remedied that deficiency by salvaging rifles and pistols, the source being "the corpses with which this district is so plentifully supplied."[11]

Not all of the 138th was to the right of the 140th. Sweningsen's battalion, in command of a lieutenant, was ordered to move west and north to Montrebeau Woods. It was the most difficult going Sweningsen had in his life. The undergrowth in the woods was so thick he had to break small trees all the way. Shells were coming in. He remembered seeing no member of his company on either side because of the undergrowth. Infantrymen obviously had gone through the woods earlier, because he saw bodies of German snipers. The snipers must have been in the upper branches of the trees, because the bodies lay below. After an hour he broke through the woods, stopped at the edge, and looked around. Ahead lay a denuded hill—nothing going on there. To his left he saw a soldier who did not see him. He could not go ahead by himself, he wrote, for this was not a one-man war. He turned back, found an aid station, had a shrapnel wound in his neck swabbed with iodine, and was sent back to a base hospital, from which he did not emerge until Armistice Day.[12]

On the left part of the Thirty-fifth's sector the Second Battalion of the 139th under Major Rieger was ahead of the line to the east of Montrebeau Woods. It was in touch with the First Battalion of the 140th, although it was a kilometer away in a woods northeast of Chaudron Farm. Germans were south and west of Montrebeau, as Ristine discovered.

The 139th was to attack at 6:30 a.m. but waited until Major O'Connor with the First Battalion of the 137th repulsed a counterattack. The attack thus commenced at 7:30. Men of the 137th went forward with the 139th. A torrent of machine-gun and artillery fire struck the line, but the men kept advancing and entered Montrebeau Woods, worked their way through (this was where Sweningsen would see the bodies), and stopped at the northern edge. Rieger was to the right.

At 3:45 p.m. the brigade commanders by mutual agreement, without Traub's intervention and probably without his knowledge, each exchanged a regiment, for it made sense to put the 140th and 138th on the right under Walker as the Provisional Seventieth Brigade, and the 139th and 137th under Nuttman as the Provisional Sixty-ninth. The rebrigading did not much matter because Walker and Nuttman could not easily communicate with the regiments. Nuttman said later that he only had contact with a battalion, not knowing where the others were.

At this time the G-2 (intelligence) officer of division headquarters, Major Parker C. Kalloch, was sent up to the front. He perhaps felt that since headquarters had no word of most of the units, there was no need for an intelligence officer there. To take his place at division headquarters, corps sent Major Bruce Magruder. The acting chief of staff, Bugge, afterward told the corps inspector that under Magruder there was more information—most of which may have been from Ralph Truman of the 140th, who was sending messages reporting what he could see and hear. Kalloch, like Hawkins, was assigned to the 137th, to a battalion. He was directed to report to Hamilton, whom he found in Montrebeau Woods about 8:00 p.m. Much of the 137th was in the woods, Hamilton thought, among the trees and bushes. Kalloch had passed a great many men just north of Baulny who had become separated from their organizations and lost. Hamilton told him to try to straighten the line and cheer the men. Kalloch could do little that night because of the darkness.[13]

The stragglers and darkness were distracting Hawkins, who had been sent up with a mandate to take over from Hamilton. Finding the colonel back in command, Hawkins attached himself to the brigade post of command of Nuttman. He looked for something to do. He, too, had seen the stragglers around Baulny and could not tell whether they were lost or trying to stay away from the front. He suspected the latter. In the darkness he became lost in the effort to find Nuttman's post of command.

The wounded were another distraction. Especially for the first night of the Thirty-fifth's attack, but also through all of the days thereafter, the wounded were suffering, and the question was what to do with the injured who were "all about us," as First Lieutenant S. O. Slaughter of Company L, 140th Infantry, afterward told the *Kansas City Star.* No litters were available.[14] The uninjured improvised litters from overcoats and blankets and carried the wounded back to the Route Nationale and other roads, some little more than tracks. That was a first step. For twenty-four hours the route was blocked above Boureuilles, with nothing getting through. After that all trucks going back from ammunition and other hauls picked up wounded, acting as ambulances. At division triages transportation was intermittent, sometimes nonexistent. Men lay there in the rain with no blankets. When trucks and the few ambulances were available, they transported the seriously wounded to the rear, beyond the field hospital at Neuvilly, to a railhead, where trains took them to base hospitals.

3

By the end of the third day the state of affairs with the Thirty-fifth Division was not at all reassuring, and the question was not so much what had caused it, for this largely was the result of poor training, but more immediately, who, upon the division's entrance into the line, was responsible.

Responsibility, it does appear, rested with three individuals, the principal one being the commander in chief, General Pershing, who in his tactical rigidity was unable to see that one set of tactics, the attack, could not fit all. He insisted that all three corps in the battle, nine divisions, attack on the morning of Friday, September 27, at 5:30 a.m. His personality was so dominant that a division commander like Traub was afraid to stand up to him. Pershing was a first-class driver. He once sat down with General Wright and displayed his commanding personality—this on October 15 when Wright's Eighty-ninth Division was about to go into the Bantheville Woods in the Fifth Corps to the right of the First and would have to put down the nightly infiltrations by which German troops hoped to squeeze the Americans out of the woods, which constituted a salient. Wright had his hands full in preparation and did not need hectoring. Pershing had known him at West Point, where they had been friends. According to Wright's chief of staff, Colonel John C. H. Lee, a World War II lieutenant general, Wright was shaking as the commander in chief pounded a table in Wright's quarters to make his points. Pershing was the friend of no one and would relieve a major general in a flash if it served his own purpose. He told Wright that night, with Lee relighting the candles on the table as the commander in chief shook

them out as he pounded, that the Eighty-ninth Division (which he pronounced first-class, to make his point easier) had to do well.[15]

When Pershing had a point to make, almost every general in his enormous command listened and perhaps shook—save the redoubtable Major
General Hunter Liggett, a big, overweight man who commanded First Corps
in the first weeks of the Meuse-Argonne. Liggett could be impassive. He
later said privately that he thought the Thirty-fifth had been pushed too far.
But he did not argue when the attack orders for September 27 came down
and told his chief of staff, Craig, to pass them to his division commanders.

Actually, Pershing's state of mind was recorded by Liggett's aide, Major
Pierpont L. Stackpole, a wise and quick-witted Boston lawyer in private life,
and it is worth stating as Stackpole related it. The commander in chief
passed through First Corps headquarters at 7:30 on Thursday evening, after
visiting the Twenty-eighth and Thirty-fifth divisions. Stackpole was not in
the room at the time, but Liggett told him about it afterward. Pershing
seemed to be in a rather excited state of mind, the major wrote, "with much
to say about the enormous importance of our operations and the possibility
of ending the war right here if they were successful and the imperative need
of drive and push." Liggett, Stackpole said, gave Pershing a notion of the
terrain, the "insidious character" of the opposition, the handicap of attacking with inexperienced divisions with a lack of training, new officers, a loss
of officers, and poor ones. The commander in chief said he appreciated this.
Liggett told Stackpole he seemed in good humor.[16]

Admittedly the attack along the line was necessary, apart from Pershing's
inclination to push. Time was running out. The German commander, Gallwitz, was doing his best—and his effort was almost as masterful as that of
Ludendorff on the entire German line from the Channel to Switzerland—
to fill the gaps in his line, the gap of the moment being in front of the
Americans in the Meuse-Argonne. Gallwitz's problem required quick thinking, and he switched his divisions as rapidly as the German motor trucks on
their flat steel rims—Germany was suffering a shortage of rubber—could
bring them in.

The unfortunate situation was that among Pershing's divisions in First
Corps the Thirty-fifth was incapable of what he desired. The order to attack
at 5:30 a.m. on Friday, September 27, did not at all suit the circumstances of
the division.

Then with an insistence that was rigid, unique to the Thirty-fifth, the
commander in chief passed down an edict that the Thirty-fifth could not

hang back, that it must do its work like everyone else, and this led Traub to order a night attack at 5:30 in the evening, a successful but tactically dangerous order, impossible without spreading out his regiments when their battalions stumbled forward in the dark. The Thirty-fifth was a delicate instrument, improperly trained, under a nearly clean sweep of new commanders arranged by the division commander at the very last moment before the battle opened.

The second individual responsible for the Thirty-fifth's plight after the evening attack of September 27 was General Traub, who did not understand people enough to learn who they were, and whose command skills could not be described as much better than posturing, hanging back, remaining remote, showing himself here and there, and then impulsively taking actions such as the dismissals of McClure and Martin before the opening attack.

But behind the facade of his jutting chin and ability to display two stars on his shoulders and carry a swagger stick (his habit when in the field), Traub was weak, unable to take a chance on his career and stand up to Pershing. If the commander in chief ordered the Thirty-fifth into battle without artillery (which Traub in his lack of grasp of the smaller facts of his division's movements may not have understood fully), that was all right: Pershing was his superior officer. As for the night attack, beginning at 5:30 p.m., he showed no judgment in allowing such a dangerous tactic. If the Thirty-fifth could show a paper position of taking territory in accord with corps and army goals, that was all right. He should have known from the corps instructions for the morning attack that General Pershing's goal, reaching Fléville, was too much for the Thirty-fifth. This should have bolstered any willingness on his part to show independence, but alas there was none. In the evening, again, spurred by Pershing's absurd message received at 4:30, he ordered an attack for an hour later.

After the night of the twenty-seventh, Traub's control of brigades and regiments virtually ceased, and he might have realized that he could not safely send the division into another attack, which he nonetheless did the next day. After the Thirty-fifth withdrew and the inspector came in, Traub himself related how poor his control had become. At noon on September 28, the division post of command, by this time having moved from the Côtes de Forimont to Cheppy, was unable to communicate by wire with either of the brigades. In explanation of the isolation of his headquarters he claimed, and it seemed as if he were blaming the staff for it, when it was his idea, that brigade commanders were at all times well forward. Walker and Nuttman, especially Nuttman, took his advice to heart. Nuttman moved his post of command so often that runners coming back with messages could not deliver them. His adjutant, Major Dwight F. Davis, and his aide, Lieutenant Sylvester Judge, warned Nuttman against this. He gave no attention.

Communication was essentially by runner. Conditions of the roads, the Route Nationale to the west along the Aire and the woods roads, were such that it was hardly possible to get motorcycles back and forth. Headquarters horses had been left behind at the beginning of the battle and for the first two days were still there. On the third day, a Saturday, Traub ordered a provisional squadron of the Second Cavalry attached to find the front line. Also on Saturday, Traub shifted the division post of command to Cheppy, but he did not stay with the post, absent on personal reconnaissance.

Control thus had become a prime issue, probably the most important factor in causing the collapse of the Thirty-fifth. Once the regiments got into the field, there was no directing hand from division. The infantry colonels were on their own.

The division commander had no idea who was responsible for the lack of liaison. "Who is responsible for the lack of coordination?" the inspector asked. "Conditions are the cause of the falling down of the coordination in this respect," was the answer.[17]

The third person responsible for what happened on the morning of September 27, although he somewhat redeemed himself that evening, was General Berry of the Sixtieth Field Artillery. There is no reason to dwell on Berry's personal inabilities, except to say that they had not helped in the training of the division when he temporarily was in command; whatever the War Department stipulated he apparently went along with. More pertinent, once the Thirty-fifth went into action, was his failure to give the division as much artillery support as possible, when its training gave it disadvantages. Support on the twenty-sixth probably was all right. That on the morning of the twenty-seventh distinctly was not. And Berry simply looked at the developing muddle over the time of attack and seems not to have done a thing about it. His headquarters was next to that of Traub, and when he learned, as surely he did, of the time discrepancy between Hawkins's attack order and that of the corps as issued by Pershing, 8:30 and 5:30, and that Traub was going to go with Pershing, he should have intervened, almost forcibly if necessary, perhaps spelling out for Traub what would happen if only a single artillery battalion got into action. Klemm of the 129th knew of the attack time by 3:00 a.m., and he knew that he had to draw up a barrage schedule and would not get done until at least 6:00. Berry does not seem to have done anything during this time except respond, as his dispositions allowed, to Traub's attack arrangements.

The reason for Berry's inertness when a crisis was shaping may itself have been personal, a result of his sensitivity to Traub's command style. Berry was Old Army and had seen many a personal contretemps and knew when warning signs were up. He knew what had happened to McClure and Martin and that Traub was possibly willing to do the same to him. In hearings after the war Traub told his auditors that if Berry had not done his will he, the commanding general, would have relieved him immediately. Berry would have sensed that fact and have been willing to see Traub fall in a hole, as was about to happen at 3:00 a.m. on the twenty-seventh, rather than take a chance personally. What this attitude amounted to was the artillery brigadier's willingness to see the infantry of his division fall in a hole. His relations with Traub were at arms' length. The two were so formal that Berry sent typed letters to Traub, and apparently the division commander reciprocated, instead of one or the other walking the several yards between the two posts. One has the impression that Berry was creating a paper record.[18]

Berry did not use aerial spotting at the outset of the action and spent his time complaining about the air service, which did nothing to improve the artillery support he gave the front-line troops. He had learned little about the importance of planes for revealing enemy positions, an art that the Germans had mastered, since he was with Pershing in Mexico in 1916. As the action of the Thirty-fifth's infantrymen continued into the division's last day on the line, September 30, he became more interested in spotting. Pershing happened by on the second day, and Berry told the commander in chief that planes were useless. His words, in the presence of the Thirty-fifth's acting chief of staff, Colonel Bugge, were, "They are no damn good."[19] He changed his mind, but his lateness did not help the division.

Berry as well as Traub needed to know where the units of the Thirty-fifth were, so he could support their artillery requests. But his relations with the First Aero Squadron were so frosty that he seems to have ignored the problem. It is true that the Thirty-fifth was delinquent in the use of panels. The aero squadron, according to the chief of the AEF air service, Major General Patrick, could never get any battalion, regimental, or brigade headquarters to identify itself. The commander of the 137th Infantry had his attention drawn to the fact that an airplane was calling for post of command panels.

Investigation showed the 137th could not find its panels anywhere around regimental headquarters. Four runners went back for them but did not bring the panels (from wherever they found them) until hours later, long after the plane had left. On September 29 runners appeared at the Thirty-fifth Division headquarters looking for panels for one of the brigades and found them in the office of the division signal officer; Wieczorek had had them, and when Olson took over he did not have time to survey his holdings and see what the office possessed. Lieutenant D'Amour, the liaison officer between the aero squadron and division headquarters, had been told on September 25 that brigades and regiments and battalions were all in possession of their panels.[20] But Berry should have seen this confusion as soon as incidents began to happen, and indeed should have checked to see if field units had their panels, for the location of units was very much his business. He does not seem to have done so, again taking refuge in letting someone else raise an issue.

Berry gave no attention to the breakdown of all divisional communication except by runners. Perhaps this was because his own telephone communication was in excellent order. From the beginning he was connected to each of his regiments, and if the wire broke, it soon was in repair. He appears to have had insulated wire. He did not pass on his wisdom in this regard, as he might have done before the battle.

A signal delinquency of Berry was in the slow rate of fire of his guns. First Lieutenant Michel Jacobs of the corps inspector's office was sent over to the Thirty-fifth by Craig, who told him the Thirty-fifth was in a "great mess" and he should get up there and check especially the artillery.[21] Jacobs attempted to tell Berry about the rate of fire of the Sixtieth Field Artillery Brigade's 75s, which was two shots a minute or less. On September 27 a total of 1,200 shells went into German positions, compared with 40,000 the day before. Berry at one point during the days in line told Jacobs a barrage was going on. The assistant corps inspector watched the guns. Not more than one shell per minute was going over, and on some guns it was every two minutes. "If there was necessity of a heavy barrage to support the infantry this was not quick time," he wrote. Jacobs's appraisal, one should add, was on the twenty-ninth when the men at the front were in extremis and needed as many shells in the air as the artillery brigade could handle. If that is what Berry's guns could handle on the twenty-ninth, it is likely that earlier, say on the morning of the twenty-seventh, they were doing less.

Berry thought two shots a minute sufficed for a light gun. Jacobs knew that at Château-Thierry in June a light gun had fired six or seven or more shots a minute, and told Berry, whose answer was that his ammunition would not allow it. The First Division history in describing the rate of fire for 75s when a First Army attack opened on October 4, the First having replaced the Thirty-fifth, related that batteries fired ten shots per minute "until the heated guns warned of their danger."[22] Jacobs could not have known this, but he also told Berry that in a battery of four it was possible to rest a gun while the other three were firing. Berry's answer was silence.

Jacobs's efforts to deal with Berry were to no avail. Jacobs reported back to corps on September 29. At that time, Craig was with General Liggett. Jacobs sent in a note saying that he was at hand and the Thirty-fifth was in a tight place, which was an understatement. He wished to know if he should report while the chief of staff was with the corps commander. Craig came to the door and said a report was not necessary, that he had arranged everything for the Thirty-fifth Division. The arrangement must have been replacement of the Thirty-fifth by the First. Jacobs prepared a report, dated October 1, in which he recommended the relief of Berry.

There was an aftermath, in which Berry got into trouble and, canny Old Army man that he was, managed to get out. He probably felt that he had some standing with Pershing, having known him well as his artillery commander during the expedition into Mexico in 1916. When the United States declared war on Germany the next year, Berry was the army's senior artillery commander. His promotion to brigadier general was not for that reason but because he was a Regular full colonel and promotion to general rank was standard for such Regulars, coming not long after the declaration of war. He had reason nonetheless to feel some confidence if criticized. After the Thirty-fifth came out of the line in the Meuse-Argonne the corps inspector began investigating, and in the conclusions to his report he criticized the handling of division artillery as unimaginative and mentioned Berry by name. First Army chief of staff Drum sent the inspector's conclusions to Traub for the enlightenment of the Thirty-fifth's officers and men. Openly embarrassed, Berry about this time learned that Lieutenant Jacobs had recommended his relief. Here was a first lieutenant recommending relief of a Regular brigadier general. He sent a letter up through channels to General Headquarters defending his brigade and himself, and cannily did so in a thicket of detail, relevant and otherwise. General Traub, aware of some of his own inadequacies, passed this hot potato (it was going to Pershing, who might defend Berry, with unfortunate personal results) to corps with his hearty support. Corps, scenting trouble and unwilling to take sides on something that was past history (and by this time General Liggett privately felt that the Thirty-fifth had been pushed too hard), mechanically passed the letter on to the First Army. On November 4, the First Army recommended to General Headquarters that Jacobs be relieved—saying he had insufficient experience to make judgments about Berry.

It is of interest that behind this careful treatment of Berry's objections to Drum's criticism was institutional memory of what he had not done with the Thirty-fifth. Between Craig and Liggett and Drum and Pershing someone spread the word. The General Headquarters inspector general, receiving Drum's recommendation for the relief of Jacobs, promoted the first lieutenant to captain. After the war many general officers were reduced to their permanent rank in the Regular Army. Berry was a permanent colonel. Because he had been the senior Regular field artillery colonel at the beginning of the war, he might have expected to hold his wartime rank, but he did not.

Whoever was responsible, the Thirty-fifth Division was in quite a predicament at the end of the third day, Saturday, September 28. Because of the dispositions of the three days, the regiments were now pretty much in a line, rather than two regiments being in place for attack, with two in support. The 138th had stretched out to cover the gap between the 140th and the Ninety-first Division. On the far left units of the 137th were in the area between the 139th and the Aire. This meant that there were no infantry regiments in reserve. The new chief of staff, Bugge, was concerned about this, as well as about the density of the men as they stood along the line. They were too obvious to the enemy. "After the evening attack when the whole division found itself in a single line," he told the corps inspector, "it would have been difficult for the Germans to fire a shot on that line without hitting someone."[23]

Terrain northeast of Boureiulles. (National Archives)

One of the craters on the road to Varennes, as seen by a military artist. (National Archives)

Varennes, as seen by a military artist. (National Archives)

Six-ton Renault light tanks attached to the Thirty-fifth Division.
(National Archives)

Prisoners. (National Archives)

Major General Peter E. Traub. (National Archives)

General Traub and a moving-picture cameraman. (National Archives)

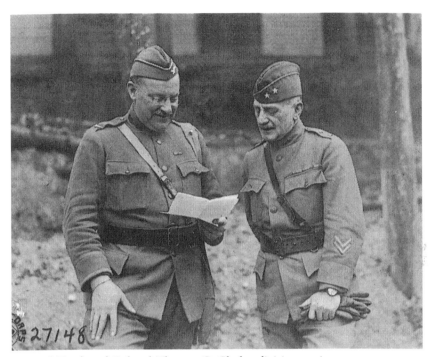

General Traub and Colonel Thomas C. Clarke, division engineer.
(National Archives)

General Traub and his staff. Colonel Hamilton S. Hawkins is to his right. (National Archives)

Brigadier General Lucien G. Berry and his staff. (National Archives)

Brigadier General Hugh A. Drum, chief of staff of the First Army.
(National Archives)

Brigadier General Charles I. Martin, commanding the Seventieth Infantry Brigade. (From Charles B. Hoyt, *Heroes of the Argonne*)

Major Dwight F. Davis. (National Archives)

Captain Harry S. Truman. This photo was taken in the summer of 1918, before the Meuse-Argonne. (Harry S. Truman Library)

Lieutenant Colonel Carl L. Ristine was promoted to full colonel after the Meuse-Argonne. (Clair Kenamore, *The Story of the 139th Infantry*, 18)

Major James E. Rieger, promoted to lieutenant colonel after the Meuse-Argonne. (Clair Kenamore, *The Story of the 139th Infantry*, 28)

Lieutenant Colonel Channing E. Delaplane, commander of the 140th Infantry. His sobriquet, of which he was proud, was Dogface Delaplane. (Evan A. Edwards, *From Doniphan to Verdun*, 56)

Major Fred L. Lemmon, First Battalion, 140th Infantry. A Regular, Lemmon was shot in the chest in the Meuse-Argonne but continued to command his battalion. (Evan A. Edwards, *From Doniphan to Verdun*, 60)

First Lieutenant John H. Pleasants, promoted to captain after the Meuse-Argonne. He was a Regular who exposed himself to machine-gun fire as he expertly handled a mortar. He was a veteran of the Boxer Rebellion and told Sergeant Triplet that only a Chinese arrow could stop him (in 1900 he had been so stopped). (Evan A. Edwards, *From Doniphan to Verdun*, 84)

Sergeant William S. Triplet, a youth of eighteen, platoon sergeant in the 140th Infantry, Meuse-Argonne. (Elizabeth T. Hennig)

Four

Sunday, September 29

I

There can be no doubt of the reason General Traub ordered an attack at 5:30 on the morning of Sunday, September 29, the attack that broke the division. On the morning before, the twenty-eighth, the chief of staff, Bugge, had proposed to Traub that the division reorganize before any more attacks. That afternoon Pershing came into division headquarters and said an attack was necessary and would happen that evening. He turned to Bugge, who was present at the time, and asked what he thought. The colonel said it could not be done that evening with any assurance of success. The commander in chief then said, "Well, make it at tomorrow morning regardless of cost."[1]

Later, on the road between Varennes and Cheppy, the chief of staff and the division machine-gun officer, Lieutenant Colonel Donald D. Hay, returning from corps headquarters, saw the army commander, and Pershing told them the Thirty-fifth Division had to attack the next morning without fail. He said the Germans were on the run and the war soon would be over.[2]

It would have been far better if there had not been an attack on Sunday morning the twenty-ninth. In the evening of the preceding day Montrebeau Woods filled with infantrymen, some together in units and some separated. It would have been possible to defend the north edge of the woods, with the men protected by the underbrush and able to fire rifles and machine guns at any German infantrymen who chose to walk across the open area from the village to the north, Exermont, and the ravine that ran westward from in front of Exermont out toward the end of the sector bordering on the Aire. The position would not have been ideal, for German shells already were finding the defenders, bringing down branches and trees. Almost any shell could threaten a soldier. But the woods might have been held. It was sizable, but the men were there.

The Germans' ability to attack and force the Americans out of Montrebeau Woods was not overwhelming. The troops in the area consisted mostly of the small—the German divisions were around three thousand men—Fifth Guards Division with assistance from remnants of the First Guards and from the German Fifty-second Division's regiments. The Germans were supported by artillery, including guns in the heights of the Argonne forest around Châtel-Chéhéry, with their pits embedded in the cement-like soil. They had command of the air.

Without knowledge of these subtleties, Pershing gave his order to Traub, who passed it on to his brigade commanders.

For the Americans there was the continuing problem of artillery support. During these opening days in the Meuse-Argonne, the U.S. Army commanders could not quite grasp what was necessary. Going into the Meuse-Argonne the AEF had known of the gigantic preparation fire and barrages of Lieutenant Colonel Georg Bruchmueller. Some of the American commanders appreciated the need of infantry for fire that would destroy or hold down opponents. Artillery had long been a specialty of the U.S. Army. At Gettysburg, the classic battle of the Civil War, Union artillery had decimated General George Pickett's line. The army could hardly ignore its achievement in 1863, and its experts kept in touch with developments abroad. The army's three-inch field gun was as good as the French 75. But the other arms appear to have taken priority. The army's three-inch gun could not be produced rapidly enough, once war was declared, and it was necessary to use French guns.

The army's artillery organization in 1917–1918, which designated one artillery brigade for each division, with two regiments of light three-inch guns and one regiment of heavy 155s, tended to persuade each division commander that one artillery brigade was enough and, moreover, if another division desired two, that was its problem. When a division went into the line for the first time it often found its artillery brigade unready, in which case it could lay claim to another division's brigade. Normally, however, each kept its own and felt satisfied.

As the Meuse-Argonne developed, it became evident that for an attack division more artillery could easily be used, and this became clear during the final attack on November 1, in which the point divisions were both in Fifth Corps, at that moment fighting only those two divisions. Each had two brigades of artillery, not one. It would be possible to lay the artillery support of the Fifth Corps's divisions on November 1 to its then commander, Summerall, whom Pershing promoted from the First Division. There can be no question that the forceful Summerall, who started with the AEF as artillery brigade commander of the Forty-second Division and believed artillery could do anything, was at least in part the architect of the attack on November 1, an artillery bombardment that in sheer fury and thoroughness surpassed anything the AEF had previously produced. For November 1 responsibility also lay with, among others, the army's artillery commander, Major General Edward C. McGlachlin. But, essentially, the result was due to experience. Neither Traub nor Berry understood the need of the infantrymen for artillery support. They did not have experience on September 29, when the artillery scheme for the division's last attack failed. One artillery brigade was not enough.

It is saddening, too, that experience was to teach the AEF artillerists to vary the nature of the shells, so that when they were trying to take out the enemy's artillery the shells would be full of high explosive, while if enemy troops were the target the necessity was shrapnel. If they could get guns close enough, flat trajectory with its ricochet was the thing, rather than hole-digging. In the early days commanders fired what they had on hand. It is true that there were supply problems in obtaining stocks for special purposes. But there was no imagination in asking for the right sort of shells at supply dumps, nor in bringing up the guns.

During the action of the Thirty-fifth Division on September 29, as on the four days that preceded, the artillery brigade used no gas shells, and there again, as in the general use of artillery, it and the other divisions learned by experience. The Germans had employed gas shells from the beginning of the Meuse-Argonne. Colonel Wieczorek was gassed the first day. It was possible to contend that a good soldier would avoid gas, and there was some truth in that argument. When the Germans were attacking American troops in Montrebeau Woods they drenched the place; all low areas, especially ravines, were dangerous, and a good infantryman could keep that point in mind. Luck, as well as care, could save men. A member of the 110th Engineer Regiment manning the hastily improvised engineers' line that would save the division on September 29 remarked in his memoir of many years later that at the time he was so glad the weather turned cold, for it kept down the gas.[3] But gas, even if controlled by the men who had to live close to it, was a terrible nuisance, and this was a part of the calculation of the German enemy that employed it. Troops in the woods were forced to stay there with masks, which were difficult to use because of trouble with breathing, and also because the circled eyeglasses fogged up.

As with artillery, AEF commanders began the Meuse-Argonne in ignorance of the need for gas to counter German gas and learned by experience. At the outset, division commanders to a man did not want any gas and flame troops in their lines sending gas, for they believed, somewhat quaintly since on the German side the genie was out of the bottle, that if they used it there would be retaliation. Sad experience taught its lesson. When Summerall's First Division relieved the Thirty-fifth on the night of September 30–October 1, one of the first things the Germans did was fill the ravines, in particular those that ran east-west and afforded shelter from artillery and most (unless well-aimed) machine-gun fire. Casualties were heavy. So when Summerall in the final First Army attack beginning November 1 commanded the Fifth Corps he asked for and obtained gas in support of his infantry. Even then, one of the Eighty-ninth Division's brigade commanders pleaded at the last minute that there be no gas. In the same attack the First Corps to the left, in need of ridding itself of enemy artillery in the large woods ahead of the attacking Seventy-eighth Division, put thousands of rounds of gas into that woods and silenced the opposing batteries.

On the morning of September 29 it was too soon in the AEF's developing understanding of gas warfare to use gas against the First and Fifth Guards divisions and the arriving German Fifty-second Division and avoid defeat of the U.S. Thirty-fifth Division. Of the quarter million Americans killed and wounded in the war, gas shells caused one-third of the casualties (shell and shrapnel half, and rifle and machine-gun fire one-tenth).

In the artillery fire that accompanied the attack on September 29, and despite the need for artillery brigadiers to have experience, Berry made several miscalculations that seem inexcusable. One was to assign the 130th Artillery Regiment of heavy howitzers a fire by the map that would stand one kilometer north of Exermont until the rolling barrage, to be fired by the 128th and 129th regiments of light guns, moved up to that line, whereupon the 130th was to lift its fire to the German batteries at Châtel-Chéhéry. A standing fire north of Exermont might have prevented the Germans from reinforcing their defenses in Exermont, on Hill 240, known as Montre-fagne, and in the Bois de Boyon on top of it. Fire on the flanking batteries in Châtel-Chéhéry might have cut down on their fire during the infantry attack. But the division's infantry available for the attack was not strong on the right-hand side of the division sector, what with the 138th weakened by stretching to the right to cover the four-kilometer gap. On the left-hand side of the Thirty-fifth's sector the 137th had disintegrated and the 139th was starting to go. Both sides were in trouble and needed every artillery piece firing in the barrage, including the heavy howitzers of the 130th.

Reducing the barrage of his brigade by one regiment, Berry assigned the 128th and 129th light regiments each 1,500 meters. The 128th, supporting the right side of the line, involving the 140th and 138th, had only a single battalion in action. That meant that, on the right fifteen hundred meters, the three batteries in the 128th's battalion each covered five hundred meters. With four guns to a battery, each gun had one hundred and twenty-five me-ters, or four hundred feet. This coverage was utterly inadequate. On the left side the 129th had two battalions firing for fifteen hundred meters, so that each battalion had to cover seven hundred and fifty meters, or two hundred and fifty meters per battery, which came to sixty meters, or two hundred feet, per gun. Even that was none too dense a coverage.

There was a third miscalculation on Berry's part. This, as one would have expected, was his guns' rate of fire. Jacobs believed they fired two shots per minute or less. The War College study says that each battery rested one gun while the others fired four shots per minute. Its estimate seems to be based on figures for shells fired that day, and those figures are not altogether clear, for they may well have been for shells on hand—in any event, to start with the number of shells and move back to the number of guns firing and the firing rate appears to be an uncertain way of calculation. After the war Colonel Klemm of the 129th told the newspaper that the guns were firing two shots per minute. That rate of fire, or four shots (one gun resting), was hardly what the 75s might have done. And there is no evidence in the War College study that there was any shortage of ammunition, despite Berry's explanation to Jacobs that he was running out.

A final miscalculation in Berry's barrage was that he began it two hun-dred meters south of Exermont. The distance from the top of Montrebeau Woods to Exermont was one thousand meters. This meant that the area in between, eight hundred meters, was not covered. During the night of September 28–29 the Germans sent machine gunners down from Exermont and covered it—against the attacking troops of the Thirty-fifth Division.

Some sort of confusion occurred in the failure to place the starting point of the barrage closer to Montrebeau. It might have been the illness of the division's operations officer, Colonel Gallagher. He had contracted pneumonia, from which he would die on October 4. It is possible that he was not thinking at all straight in stipulating in the division field order, number 48, that the barrage should start just south of Exermont. It is barely possible, for he was at Cheppy, that he did not know the troops had taken Montrebeau, although this seems unlikely. He may have felt that it was better not to start a barrage closer to the troops and chose two hundred meters south of Exermont (eight hundred north of Montrebeau) as a safer distance, so there would be no short fire.

It is possible that General Berry, at Cheppy with Gallagher, let the latter do what he wished, not calling his attention to the fact that his artillery was good enough to fire two hundred meters above the troops' starting line. Berry might have been observing his habit of keeping out of division (that is, Traub's) business. It is a curious fact that when the division orders came out at 10:00 p.m. on September 28, Berry misread them and set his barrage two hundred meters north of Montrebeau, at 80.0. He then sent a correction, two and one-half hours later, putting the opening of the barrage two hundred meters south of Exermont, at 80.6, as the division order read.

In this last regard one might say, again, that because Berry had good wire and was in easy contact with his regiments he could have known better than Traub where the front line was on the morning of September 29. Perhaps he did not wish to know.

2

On both sides of the division front the attack scheduled for 5:30 a.m. on September 29 was a disaster. The weather was bad, which probably had nothing to do with the success or failure of the attack, but it did not raise the spirits of the attackers. It was dark and cold, with a drizzle that turned to driving rain.

The attack orders were clear enough, a model of what orders ought to be. They called for a rolling barrage by the two regiments of 75s, the 128th and 129th regiments, to start two hundred meters below Exermont. The 130th Field Artillery Regiment was to put a curtain of fire above Exermont on

Montrefagne, Hill 240 containing the Bois de Boyon, and hold it until the
rolling barrage came up, whereupon the 130th would shift fire to the Argonne.
On both the right-hand and left-hand sides of the division sector a single
infantry regiment was scheduled to attack—the 138th on the right, the 137th
on the left. On the right the 140th would be in support, on the left the
139th. The brigades were to be in column, the Provisional Seventieth Brigade under Walker on the right, the Sixty-ninth under Nuttman on the left.
At the far left of the left-hand line a squadron of cavalry would maintain
liaison with the Twenty-eighth Division across the Aire in the vicinity of
Apremont. Tanks would be out in front all along the line.

The plan was clear enough. But at the outset of the attack on the right-
hand part of the division sector a difficulty developed involving delivery of
the attack orders: they came too late to allow the infantry to get behind the
barrage. Because Pershing had told Traub and Bugge and Hay the day before that the Thirty-fifth had to attack, headquarters started preparing
the attack orders for the brigades to pass on to the regiments, well before
the corps sent orders at 11:00 p.m. spelling out what the Thirty-fifth was to
do. The division order went out at 10:00 p.m. The Provisional Sixty-ninth
Brigade order went out at 2:30 a.m. and reached Colonel Delaplane of the
140th Regiment at 5:25, five minutes before the rolling barrage. Colonel
Parker of the 138th Regiment received the Seventieth Brigade order at 6:45
or 7:00 a.m.

The barrage moved out promptly at 5:30, and no troops followed. A barrage had a morale-building effect, with the troops behind believing they
had a curtain in front of them, and so there was to be no morale building on
the right-hand part of the division sector. Presumably a barrage put the defending troops in a state of shock, and if strong enough would drive them
to cover, whence if the infantry was close enough behind the barrage the attackers could surprise them, and this aspect of the barrage also was lost.

After the difficulty over receiving orders—in which half a day proved
necessary, between Pershing's visit to the Thirty-fifth Division's sector and
the time of attack, to draw up and disseminate orders—the division require-
ment that the 138th attack and the 140th be in support produced another
problem.

With five minutes to organize his support line before the barrage, Delaplane had his hands full; indeed, he could not manage in that time and
needed another hour. The 140th had been holding a line of eight hundred
meters, with two battalions in line and one in support. The 138th lay some-

what behind it, with two companies attempting to fill the gap to the right between the Thirty-fifth Division and the Ninety-first. Delaplane started his arrangements for his regiment's support role, behind the 138th, the formation ordered being for the 140th to move in column by battalions, with the First (Captain John W. Armour) and Second (Major Warren L. Mabrey) in the front line and the Third (Major Murray Davis) in support.

By 6:25, the barrage long since having gone, Delaplane was moving his battalions around into the order stipulated by the division plan, preparing for his support role, when he suddenly learned that he was to attack—this because the 138th, not having received its orders, was nowhere in sight. The manner in which he learned it emphasized how botched the morning attack turned out.

After the action Delaplane described what happened. The division chief of staff, Hawkins, deputized by Traub to take over the 137th Infantry or do anything else to straighten out battlefield command, and his place at division headquarters taken by Bugge, was on the scene and turned to Delaplane and said, in regard to the 138th Regiment, "As long as they are not here you will advance." Delaplane protested that "if that was the case I would like a little time to straighten out things so as to get out." Hawkins said something to the effect that if the men of the 140th would get out of their shell holes they might be able to move forward. Nuttman, who was commanding the Provisional Sixty-ninth Brigade containing what was left of the 137th and 139th regiments, also was at Delaplane's command post—he should have been over to the left of the division sector—and supported Hawkins's demand that the 140th take the place of the 138th. At this juncture the Provisional Seventieth Brigade commander, Walker, Delaplane's own superior, came up. Delaplane turned to him, relating the attack orders, which said that the 138th would attack. At that moment Delaplane thought he saw the 138th's men beginning to come up, and pointed this out to Hawkins, Nuttman, and Walker. But it was a case of a lieutenant colonel telling something to three full colonels. Walker agreed with the others.

Hawkins said something to the effect that if things were not as he decided he would relieve Delaplane. According to Delaplane, "I replied that if things were going to be handled in that manner he could relieve me whenever he saw fit."

Out of the corner of his eye Delaplane then saw that someone had alerted one of his battalions, the Third, and it was moving forward. There was no point in further protest, and he went forward to accompany his men. He later spoke with the commander of the Third, Davis, who told him that Hawkins had ordered the battalion forward. Davis was killed at 10:00 a.m. at Exermont, and there was no way to prove this gross assumption of Delaplane's authority, about which he was still angry when the division, including what was left of his regiment, came out of the line.[4]

Someone also ordered up the 138th, even though Parker did not receive his orders from the brigade until later. As in the case of the Third Battalion of the 140th, it was impossible to verify who sent up the 138th, because in the attack that morning Parker was killed.

And so, on the right-hand side of the division sector, the officers and men of the 140th went forward. It was a poised moment. When Delaplane joined his advancing troops the 140th was down to a thousand men, from the three thousand or more with which he had begun the battle. It is unclear how many of them moved down the slope toward the creek and into Exermont. When he reached Exermont, he had four hundred men. When he had passed through this village of a little more than a few houses and a church, he had six. A hundred more came up shortly.

Delaplane at Exermont was joined at 10:00 a.m. by Major Rieger of the Second Battalion of the 139th. Two days before, during the night attack, Rieger's battalion had gotten to the east of Montrebeau. By the morning of September 29 the major had two depleted companies. As he was moving forward to reinforce Delaplane he came across Nuttman, who gave him wrong directions for getting into the attack line, preventing him from passing through Montrebeau Woods as he wished to do, and the misinformation—Nuttman insisted on the course he recommended—forced him into the open and much weakened his two companies. Along the way he picked up two depleted companies of the 140th. At last moving out toward Exermont he found the attack—of course without a barrage—most difficult, as he afterward wrote his wife. Being a religious man he watched to see if religion was moving the men, and he assured his wife that it indeed was. He said that the men remembered hymns of their youth and not merely sang but shouted them as they went forward. It was "the shout of combat, a mighty roar."[5]

Above Exermont the two officers, Delaplane and Rieger, with those men who had survived the attack, faced a hell of machine-gun fire and artillery from the Germans who were gathering for an attack at Montrefagne, Hill 240, crowned by the Bois de Boyon. The German Fifty-second Division was coming into the line to reinforce the dwindling First Guards Division and the Fifth Guards. Delaplane asked for reinforcements. None came. At

1:00 p.m. an order to retire arrived from Walker of the Provisional Seventieth, and the men went back, slowly, shell hole by shell hole, with Delaplane at the rear firing at the oncoming enemy with bursts from a Chauchat.

All this does not capture the experience of the attacking men as they sought to make the distance to wherever they were going, in the instance of the 140th down the slope to the creek, thence to Exermont, if possible through the village to the farthest point where Delaplane and Rieger lay. The narrative of Sergeant Triplet best shows what happened.

Triplet, in the First Battalion, was in charge of the second platoon, fifty men, of D Company, there being no second lieutenant. He had taken the platoon through the months from its organization at Doniphan in the autumn of 1917; he had known them for a year. He liked the men, and they admired him. It was, he afterward wrote, "in damned good shape . . . an outfit any man would be proud to be in." During the Meuse-Argonne attack of the division he held the platoon together for four days, pretty much without casualties, and actually gained a few stragglers, good men, although he did not know their names or units. He had taken the platoon through all sorts of terrain and at one point saw an enemy battalion, he thought what was identified after the war as the Wedel Battalion, slowly going south. He placed his men with care, riflemen and grenadiers and Chauchat gunners, and waited until Wedel or whoever commanded the battalion brought it within range. His platoon riddled the battalion, leaving dozens of dead and wounded, perhaps (he thought) preventing some counterattack.

On that grim morning of the twenty-ninth when the sergeant's platoon went forward with the regiment it was raining, as had been true throughout most of the division's days in the Meuse-Argonne. Triplet spread out the platoon—there was a long line to cover. Everyone wondered what it would be like to make it down a thousand meters of open country, more than half a mile, against machine guns and artillery. The rain was coming down hard, driving, and the men bent forward against it, perhaps also seeking to present smaller targets. The latter purpose, if that was why they did it, was impossible, he remembered, for it would have taken four helmet thicknesses to stop a bullet. He found himself bending forward too.

The machine guns were bad enough, the artillery worse. Mud was boiling under the machine-gun fire. But the men couldn't even hear the bullets because of the din of the shells, what the Germans described as *Trommelfeuer*, a deafening roar. Here part of the problem was that the enemy was mixing ordinary high explosive with gas, and some of Triplet's men were wearing the mouthpieces of their masks, with the apparatus itself hanging down. The sergeant was more concerned by the 77s, the German equivalent of 75s, which were firing flat-trajectory, so that the shell came in straight, rather than in the civilized way that dug holes. With flat trajectory the mud fountained out in front and the shell bounced up to burst practically under the men's helmet brims. The ricochet did it. The shell was a man-killer.

As the sergeant watched, his men fell, going down one by one. They crumpled, without heroics, just falling and disappearing. It was impossible to go to their aid, as that would lead to more casualties. He hoped that litter bearers, if there were any, or first-aid men with blankets or overcoats, would find them. The men he had known since Doniphan went down. The platoon had mustered two Indians, nicknamed Big Chief and Little Chief, whom Triplet suspected of volunteering for the army so they could kill white men, any white men. At Camp Mills on Long Island where rough so-called restaurants and bars lined the encampment and infantrymen regularly got into fights, men from an Alabama regiment cast aspersions at Triplet's men who were in the company of Big Chief and Little Chief. Big Chief looked impassively at a southerner, who thought it was possible to attack him and did so. Big Chief did a reverse headlock on the southerner and disposed of him. Triplet's entire platoon entered the fray and cleaned up on their opponents. Before the attack on the morning of the twenty-ninth the two Indians, ordinarily not talkative, were less so. Triplet thought they had decided their time had come. It did, before Exermont. He saw them crumple, like the rest of their friends. He never heard what happened to them, whether they survived, but instinctively he knew they were dead.[6]

Triplet himself fell, struck in his helmet by a bullet that did not enter but caused a concussion. For a while he could not think, then wanted only to stay down and rest. After the tumult ceased, with the rain still driving, able to think, he discovered that he had been gassed, also wounded in the shoulder. Together with one of his sergeants who had a broken leg he walked and limped for half a mile or a mile, he did not know, as both men were in a daze, back to a triage, thence to a dressing station where he and his sergeant parted, Triplet limping back to a railroad station where he lay for hours before, almost miraculously, finding himself on a hospital train bound for a base hospital. The man in the upper bunk did not look well when he was slid in; he was bleeding, the blood coming down through the blanket and bunk. The next morning he was passed over by the attendants rousing the men. They did not have time, because of the need to remove the walking wounded from the train, to carry out a body.

At the base hospital Sergeant Triplet found that his head felt better; the concussion had worn off. The gas caused a huge boil to develop on his chest, which a surgeon lanced. He had a shoulder wound that might have been the result of a rifle rather than a machine gun, as he at first thought because of facing all the machine guns. He had a knee wound, which was not surprising, although he did not know why. Colonel Henry J. Reilly of the Forty-second Division, commanding one of the Forty-second's artillery regiments and then its Eighty-third Infantry Brigade, was stationed in the vicinity of Exermont after the Thirty-fifth and its successor the First Division had come and gone, and made an interesting discovery. Bodies of Thirty-fifth Division men were still strewn around unburied when the Forty-second came up in mid-October, and Reilly noticed that within a short distance of machine-gun nests these men had been shot through the ankles and shins and through the tops of their heads. He noticed that the machine guns had not been placed on the military crest at Exermont but pushed forward in front. The Germans had surprised the Thirty-fifth's infantrymen by shooting low, through the legs and ankles, and when the men fell they were shot through the tops of their heads.[7] Fortunately, Triplet was spared the latter experience by the bullet that struck his helmet tangentially and gave him the concussion but did not enter.

The 138th, which had appeared to be coming up when Hawkins started the advance of the 140th, attacked considerably later, around 8:30. It was appallingly weak in strength. Parker had reported the Third Battalion as numbering 421; the Second, 250; and the First, 182; for a total of 859. Companies were similarly weak, some with only 30 men. The regimental intelligence officer reported the men in very poor condition and spirits.

The 138th thereupon collapsed. It went forward with its Third Battalion on the right, its Second on the left, and its First in support. The Third, under Captain Fred Bottger, advanced trying to find and pass through the 140th as in the orders and bore west of north. Bottger was gassed and eventually wandered into the lines of the Ninety-first Division. Captain Harry W. Thompson took command and suspended the advance, asked for further orders, and reorganized the lines. The Second Battalion under Lieutenant William H. Leahy, who had been Sweningsen's commander (Sweningsen was on his way to a base hospital), went forward to the left and reportedly reached the Bois de Boyon on top of Hill 240, although this seems impossible. The Second also did not connect with the 140th. The First Battalion (Lieutenant Lloyd O. Brightfield) followed the Third, west of north. Colonel Parker, accompanying, was killed at about 10:00. Captain Thompson of the Third, the senior officer on the ground, took command of the regiment, or at least as much of it as he could discover. He retained command until late that afternoon when Major Comfort, who had been on detached service at division headquarters, could rejoin. By then the remnants of the First and Second battalions were mostly behind the engineers' line that ran along the Baulny ridge. Practically, the command of the 138th Regiment on September 29 by a captain was of no large importance, as Thompson during all that time controlled only the Third Battalion.

On the left side of the division line the attack order reached the Provisional Sixty-ninth Brigade under Nuttman at 12:45, thence it went to the regiments. The 137th Regiment and a remnant of the 139th took part in the attack. The 137th's men did not get farther than the ravine west of Exermont, containing a creek that ran from the village. For a short time there was a connection between the left and right portions of the division line, but it was tenuous and disappeared. Primarily the attack on the left was the work of Major Kalloch, the division intelligence officer, who like Hawkins had been sent up to the 137th to see what he could do—which at the outset had been nothing.

Kalloch's part in what happened was for a while lost to view in some of its details, for he was on assignment away from the division, but in June 1919, upon a request from the War Department, he sent a long description, a copy of which is now in the papers of General Drum at the Army War College at Carlisle Barracks, Pennsylvania.[8] The War College study of the division had the advantage of Kalloch's firsthand account but did not quote it. The original is vivid and displays the scene of the time, though composed months later.

"At 4:20 a.m. Sept. 29th," Major Kalloch wrote, "the colonel sent for me and showed me an order he had to attack at 5:30." The colonel was Hamilton of the 137th, back in command. The brigade order stated that the 137th should form with two battalions in attack and one in support and go forward at the appointed time. As mentioned, there was to be a squadron of cavalry at the left to maintain liaison with the Twenty-eighth Division across the Aire in the vicinity of Apremont. On the right a regiment of infantry (the 138th) would go forward, another regiment following (the 140th) at a thousand meters. Tanks would be out in front of the 137th and 138th.

There would be a rolling barrage (128th and 129th Field Artillery regiments) and stationary fire (130th Regiment of 155s).

In view of what Hamilton, nominal commander of the 137th, had on hand, odd groups not necessarily of his regiment scattered all the way back through Montrebeau Woods, the attack order was totally unrealistic in its proposed panoply of attack regiments and support regiments, artillery barrage and stationary fire from the 60th Field Artillery Brigade, and the addition of cavalry and tanks. It displayed an orderly world of assignments of units and maneuvering that was parade-ground material. Kalloch and Hamilton knew that. "The colonel directed me to go down and organize the attack. I told him that it was impossible as directed in the order, due to a lack of time and the disorganization of the units, but that I would go down and do the best I could."

With that, Kalloch plunged into the woods to see what he could find and marshal for an attack in a little more than an hour, facing the darkness of the night and the thickness of the woods. Whatever unit commanders he found, he told them to get their men together and bring them up to the top of the woods. How effective that was is difficult to know. Officers hearing advice early in the morning—the time was between 4:20 and 5:30 a.m.— and from a strange major might well have dragged their feet, doing little more than going through the motions of waking and sending up men, if they knew where their men were. A guide took Kalloch to a machine-gun unit in the woods, and he told the officer to get his guns on the north edge of the woods as soon as possible. These would have been heavy guns, no Chauchats, capable of serious work with any German light machine gunners in front of the woods. What happened with the heavy guns he never learned, for they were not there when his men went forward.

On coming back up to the north edge the major ran the small line of men he had accumulated as quickly as possible, "putting the men out into position for the attack. Just before zero hour, at 5:30 a.m., I had two lieutenants and about 125 men, including two automatic rifles." The Chauchats had three or four clips of ammunition apiece. Kalloch had to cover a front of a kilometer, three-fifths of a mile, with a force so thin the enemy ahead must have wondered if it was more than a few men wandering forward. He placed a hundred in front and twenty-five in a second line, the latter almost invisible to anyone save himself, knowing they were there. The second line was to follow at fifty meters. He sent patrols of half a dozen men to the right and left and assigned lieutenants to each side of the line to maintain liaison with any troops they might discover. Lieutenant Allen commanded the right of the detachment and Lieutenant Hodgson the left.

At zero hour the men heard six shells go over from Berry's light artillery. "I thought that the barrage had commenced and started to move forward, but the fire ceased immediately and there was no further artillery support on the Sixty-ninth Brigade front during the rest of my attack." The shells must have been ranging shots, whereupon the 75s went on up to two hundred meters before Exermont, where Berry had decided to begin his barrage.

After the shots Kalloch waited four minutes and took the lines forward without any barrage. About one hundred fifty meters ahead he saw trouble. In the dim light he saw groups of light machine gunners. They allowed the first line to advance to within a hundred meters, and then the whole line of outposts opened fire. The major gave the signal to lie down and commence firing "but soon discovered that it was a losing proposition to fight rifles against machine guns in the open." He signaled the men to go forward and drive the gunners out of their positions.

The left of the first line managed the task. On the right several enemy machine guns were on the flank doing damage. He strengthened the right, to no result, and finally had to refuse—give up—that part of the line, with the left and the center continuing as far as the ravine.

There, in the ravine, the Kalloch force occupied a small ditch beyond a band of barbed wire one hundred twenty-five meters from the village, with the line extending to the west five or six hundred meters. Germans were on the near edge of the village and in a small draw on the Americans' right flank. Kalloch sent two runners back to Hamilton to tell where he was and say they could go no farther without support.

By this time Hamilton had gathered a support line, but it proved no support at all. It consisted of a hundred men whom he had gotten together and prepared to take out himself when he discovered that Major O'Connor of the Second Battalion, who had dropped out the day before from exhaustion, had come back to duty, without his battalion, and he passed the command to him. O'Connor took out the men at 6:15, and they got as far as a few hundred yards. Kalloch later questioned one of the support-line officers who said the fire was simply too hot, it was impossible to go farther.

O'Connor, crusty as ever, years later disputed Kalloch's account of what happened to his, the support, line. When he wrote to the Battle Monuments Commission about how Colonel Ristine had broken up the 137th Regiment by leapfrogging it with the 139th, he added some strictures about

Kalloch's actions on September 29. He described Kalloch as a headquarters major. He said that as he, O'Connor, was leading out his support line the center and right suddenly buckled, and the reason was that Kalloch, in front, had sent his men back. He said that if Kalloch had remained, the ravine west of Exermont could have been held.[9]

The times involved here do not support O'Connor's contention. The O'Connor line moved out at 6:15. Kalloch said that he held the ravine line in front of Exermont until 7:30, when enemy gunners were on his right and working around toward the rear. He was getting machine-gun fire from Hill 240 and artillery fire from the northwest, the enemy batteries high up in the Argonne. The Twenty-eighth Division was just north of Apremont, and German artillery was firing from above its lines. The attack regiment of the Provisional Seventieth Brigade, the 140th on the right-hand part of the division sector, was at least two kilometers to the east. There was only one recourse. "To keep from being cut off completely and considering the fact that my men had little ammunition left I decided to return to the wood." The men went back beginning at 7:30, arriving at Montrebeau around 8:00, but not before the enemy fire became so fierce that they had to jump from shell hole to shell hole to avoid being blown away.

In writing of all this months later Kalloch was asked what his casualties were. He had no idea. The men were not in any organized units, probably coming from half a dozen companies. "I never saw them before and with the exception of one lieutenant wouldn't know them on sight." What happened to his men was not pleasant to contemplate. It was bad enough to be moving out of Montrebeau without the morale-building factor of Berry's barrage, which because the commander of the Sixtieth Field Artillery Brigade began it so far forward, two hundred meters below Exermont, could not even be heard. Worse, Kalloch's men had to root out the German machine gunners that the barrage left untouched. Then, coming back from the ravine another awkwardness arose. It was impossible to bring back the wounded, given the hotness of the German machine-gun and artillery fire. They had to be left. The operations journal of the First Division described what happened to them. "The field between the Exermont ravine and our jump-off line," the journal related, "is covered with the dead bodies of men from the Thirty-fifth Division which fell back across it." The account said that many of these men had on first-aid bandages, showing they had been wounded and later died. The Germans, the journal explained, did not look after American wounded.[10]

At 3:00 a.m., the attack order reached the command post of the 139th Infantry at Baulny, where Colonel Americus Mitchell was in command, replacing Ristine, who had worked his way out to the Twenty-eighth Division earlier that morning but not yet gotten back to the Thirty-fifth's sector. Mitchell consulted his brigade commander, Nuttman, whose headquarters were close, and went up with the only part of the regiment he controlled, a few companies of the First Battalion. He picked up men as he went through the woods and reached the top with probably four hundred. At that point O'Connor's support line was falling back to the woods and passed through Mitchell's force. Kalloch's men were still in the ravine, but it was too late to reinforce him, the enemy machine guns and artillery fire being too strong.

3

At this point in the valiant but futile attacks on the morning of Sunday, September 29, it was a matter of *sauve qui peut,* the question being how far back to put a new division line. The decision was made for the Baulny ridge, a line going northeast from that village. This meant giving up Montrebeau Woods.

The governing reason for giving up the woods was General Traub's complete lack of knowledge of what was going on. He probably made the decision before the infantry actions of that morning. He went up to the southeastern edge of Montrebeau Woods and was there from midnight until 5:30. The woods were being heavily shelled and seemed no place to make a stand, and that could have persuaded him to move the line back—even before his men on both sides of the division line, then fronted by the woods, tried to take the line farther according to division orders.

It is possible that Traub was up at the front later, but the War College study, highly reliable, does give the time as midnight until 5:30. He may have decided on a fall-back line without then deciding to give up Montrebeau. This is unclear from the record.

When the front-line troops attacked and failed he still could have kept Montrebeau Woods if he had known the situation. He said afterward that he knew nothing. He could not weigh the question of whether to hold a line at the top of Montrebeau Woods against whether to place it on the Baulny ridge. He did not know that the 138th, if broken, still had men above the top of the woods, albeit to the east. After the troops went back to the engineers' line he would find out that a remnant of the Third Battalion of the

138th under Captain Thompson was still in advance of the woods line to the east, and when the First Division relieved the Thirty-fifth the First's men found Thompson's group up there. When Traub went up he does not appear to have realized that the woods were full of men in various stages of disorganization who might have been gathered. If he had known, later in the morning, that Mitchell was getting four hundred men forward, that might have made a difference. Brigadier General Nolan, General Headquarters G-2, who had a wide knowledge of the Meuse-Argonne and had been in the Thirty-fifth's sector at the beginning of the battle, spent several years in the early 1930s trying to analyze what happened in the several attacks of the six-week battle. He composed a massive memoir that he sought to publish, to no avail. He concluded therein that the loss of Montrebeau Woods occurred because of a mixing of troops. The mixing was true enough but need not have been conclusive. What was lacking were controlling hands to gather these men, as Mitchell had done. It might have been attempted.[11]

It is of interest in regard to General Traub's decision to pull the division line back that on the night before the division attacked, the general had held a meeting of the senior officers and there not merely said that commanders should be up at the front leading their men, perhaps taking fire themselves. He said, and it seems a shocking thing, but that evening before the battle the officers were terribly serious and he passed this off, that anyone who gave an order to retreat should be shot on the spot.[12]

Nonetheless, the decision was taken to go back, which allowed the German infantry to "march" into the woods the next morning, as a German writer related in describing the American retreat in *Liberty* magazine.[13] They did not march, could not have marched, in all that underbrush. But they filled the woods with machine-gun nests, and the First Division had a real fight on its hands when it sought to, and did, pry them out.

The decision to retreat to another line may have been because of the availability of a large body of men, twelve hundred of them, in the 110th Engineer Regiment, an integral unit of the division. The colonel of the regiment had been assigned to division headquarters, brought in by Traub as division engineer. This was Thomas C. Clarke, whom Kenamore described as "a plump and pleasant gentleman officer."[14] Clarke had the only large body of troops not in the line. The regiment was not altogether fresh, but it was fresh enough. There had been plenty of tasks for the engineers during the move forward of seven and one-half kilometers and the taking and attempted holding of Exermont. It had not had to fix the craters between Boureuilles and Varennes; corps engineers had been assigned to that problem. The corps had borrowed part of the engineer regiment of the Ninety-second Division, the African American unit on the far end of the Argonne, two infantry battalions of which Pershing had allowed to take part in the attack of September 26. Thus, while the infantry of the Ninety-second had been sent in as labor troops, part of the Ninety-second's engineer regiment was helping the corps engineers. The 110th Engineer Regiment had been busy with the ruts, holes, and the general falling apart of the smaller roads. It had not been in combat and suddenly needed to be. Traub designated Clarke as what one of his regiment's men described as "field divisional commanding officer."[15] Clarke sent word up to his senior battalion commander, Major Edward M. Stayton of Independence, Missouri, to put the two engineer battalions on a new division line along the Baulny ridge.

This was not the sole case in the Meuse-Argonne where engineer troops became fighting troops. The First and Forty-second divisions used them that way. In each instance the engineers were at hand and thrown in.

Stayton gathered up the two battalions and threw them into the new line. After talking to Clarke at division he telephoned Captain Orlin Hudson and told him to get his battalion up there. Private Joseph N. Rizzi remembered, perhaps with a little exaggeration, how Hudson turned to the men and with "a roar of command, a wave of his hand" shouted, "Engineers—follow me! Come let's go! Doubletime!" The object was "that trench two hundred yards away," in front of the wire.[16] What Rizzi remembered was too long and elaborate to have been the words of the captain, but Hudson surely said something of the sort.

If the Baulny ridge was not the ideal place to hold back the Germans, it was good enough. The line was a little in front of the ridge, on the line from l'Esperance to Chaudron Farm to Hill 231, with a second line on the ridge. It had no natural growth of trees and shrubs. Defenders scrambled into shell holes and foxholes dug by once-advancing infantrymen. The line was far enough back to be protected from flank fire from the Ninety-first Division sector and that of the Twenty-eighth.

The infantry came back without organization, in twos, threes, and fours. The last of the regiments, that of Delaplane, had been cut to pieces at Exermont. Battalions and companies had disappeared. The corps inspector asked Nuttman about the organization of the retreating men, whether they had any. "There was none whatever," was the answer.[17]

From the ridge line the division's few remaining officers had a place to catch men coming back. Lieutenant Colonel John C. Montgomery of First Corps staff and Major Comfort helped stop them and get them into the engineers' line. Most of them were quite willing to help with the new line, having not known what to do.

Many men were south of Baulny and the ridge line, around Charpentry, and some were stragglers and defiant. Colonel Delaplane, back on the engineers' line, put Ralph Truman near Charpentry and told him to round them up. The cousin of Harry Truman was the right man for that job. A rumor had started of a supposed order to retreat farther; the men had begun to break and run, and it was turning into a stampede. The 140th's intelligence officer got up on a small nearby hill, took out his gun, and announced that he would shoot the first man who passed him.[18]

Stayton and Hudson with their battalions of engineers, together with infantrymen gathered by Montgomery, Comfort, and Ralph Truman, were enough to save the day.

After the war Stayton went on to other things, and it is possible to say that he had a good deal to do with the making of a president of the United States. In the 1920s Harry S. Truman, the presiding judge (that is, the principal county commissioner) of Jackson County, the county comprising Independence to the east and Kansas City to the west, chose Stayton as part of a two-man engineer team (the other was a Kansas City engineer) to survey the county's roads and draw up a plan that would put every resident including rural residents within two miles of a fine cement road. General Stayton (he became a major general in the Missouri Guard) was the man for that, as Truman knew from what he had done a few years before in the Meuse-Argonne. The new roads compared only to the roads in Wayne County, the county of Detroit, and in Westchester County next to New York City. They made Judge Truman's reputation as a county executive and opened the way to his becoming a senator from Missouri, vice president of the United States, and president.

Ralph Truman, like Stayton, did well in later life. He had an interesting background. During the Spanish-American War he had brought together an unorganized group of men and without commission placed himself at its head as a sort of chairman. He took his group to Tampa and bluffed his way to Cuba. There is evidence that in 1901, in the company of his younger cousin Harry, he took a side-door Pullman, a freight car, from Missouri to Texas to visit another cousin. Before the World War he was a police detective in Kansas City, no gentle pursuit, and quit the force to go to the Mexican border. After the war he removed to Springfield and worked for the St. Louis and San Francisco Railroad. He remained in the Guard and like Stayton became a major general, and when the Thirty-fifth Division was called into federal service in 1940, which with reinstitution of a national draft helped the army prepare for World War II, he was its commander. Not long before Pearl Harbor the Guard generals of almost all divisions were relieved. Ralph Truman went with the others, perhaps the greatest disappointment of his life.

Back in 1918, the 110th manned the engineers' line, and the first glimmer of organization in the division was a message sent by Stayton:

> From CO 1st Bn., 110th Eng. at Foret Argonne 03.3.77.64, 29 Sept. 9:35 a.m. I am moving this bn. forward to draw one kilometer south of this post. P.C. will be at 030.780.[19]

Things shortly were so well in hand that Sergeant Sam W. Cobb of the headquarters detachment, 110th Engineers, from St. Louis—who when at Cheppy had worked through the night on a heavy machine gun the Germans left, disabled, until he could use it the next day against enemy airplanes—took his detachment forward, above the line, to show the stragglers that the line was in depth. By the next morning, September 30, with fifteen hundred men on the line, there was no question of its strength. A message went back from Hudson that used a Missouri simile: "We can hold this hill until the cows come home."[20]

The engineers and the others held until the night of September 30–October 1, when the Big Red One, the First Division, the pride of the AEF, under Summerall, came up.

The crisis had been so severe that the First Corps alerted its reserve division below the Twenty-eighth, the Eighty-second. The danger of the Thirty-fifth's caving in appears in the diary of the artillery brigade commander of the Eighty-second, Charles D. Rhodes, an attractive man, a West Pointer, who on the morning of Sunday, September 29, was writing letters when the word came.

> Cloudy and muddy. . . . About 12:30 noon, received telephone orders from the 82nd Division to be ready to march at 2:00 p.m. The brigade was ready at that hour, all packed up and "rarin' to go!" Horses were even

harnessed to guns and caissons. But no further word came from the division, and by repeated 'phoning, we found that the entire division was on the "alerte!" Finally, I went to division headquarters with Beere, and found that the Thirty-fifth Division has been pretty roughly handled today,—some battalions being reduced to 200 men. So, it seems, our division was placed in readiness, awaiting further orders. Finally, it was decided to send the 327th Infantry in motor trucks to fill the gap in the front lines, holding the rest of the division in readiness. Tonight we are at the "alerte," and I have men bivouacking near their guns. My adjutant is sleeping near the telephone.[21]

The Eighty-second only sent up the one regiment to the Thirty-fifth's left flank between Apremont and Baulny.

While the engineers' line was being set up, the First Army's artillery went into action. This had not happened earlier because the Thirty-fifth had not asked for artillery assistance. At 4:00 p.m., Brigadier General Dwight E. Aultman, commanding the First Army artillery in the First Corps area, reported by telephone to First Army artillery headquarters that his guns were in action and sending shells into the vicinity of Châtel-Chéhéry. He had sixteen batteries of 155-mm guns. By the evening of September 29, the First Army had doubled the guns to thirty heavy batteries. They not merely went after Châtel-Chéhéry but placed a protective arc of fire around the front and left flanks of the Thirty-fifth.[22]

Five

Aftermath

Nothing much worthy of mention happened during the last day the Thirty-fifth Division was in line, Monday, September 30. The big guns of the First Army took care of the German batteries. The engineers' line solved the division's problem with the German infantry. The division machine-gun officer, Colonel Hay, had plenty of guns in the line. The men in the series of shell holes and foxholes, with the small line of Sergeant Cobb in front, were as tired as they could be, and the weather was cold and the rain continued to descend. The enemy made sorties from Montrebeau Woods, and their planes came over and sought to rake the line. But everything was far better than it had been the day before. On the right and left flanks of the division sector the Ninety-first and Twenty-eighth were up, so there was no enfilading fire from just above their lines.

That night the First Division came in and took over, and the men of the Thirty-fifth gave the First's officers and men the tasks that had afflicted them for five long days of advance and retreat and the holding of what they believed was all that was possible.

Then, dimly at first, as if it were a sort of shadow, a strange kind of miasma, controversy arose about what the Thirty-fifth Division had done and not done.

When the division came out of the line and reformed, prior to moving to the Verdun sector, where it occupied a quiet line until near the end of the war, the officers and men were still rubbing their eyes over what had happened. Time was necessary to understand it. For the most part they felt that they had done all right. They knew that few if any of the divisions in the opening days of the Meuse-Argonne had done what had been expected of them. The First Army had made absurd overestimates of how far the divisions might go on the first days. Especially was this true about getting beyond the German second line from Grandpré to Landres-et-St. Georges, on east to the Meuse. It is possible that if division commanders had shoved their men harder, pushed them as rapidly as possible on the first day, they might have gotten up toward the First Army objective before the enemy brought in reinforcements and made further rapid movements impossible. But the work of going forward had been difficult, especially for the green divisions. When the Thirty-fifth went five kilometers on the first day, this was more than could have been expected, and the troops felt that this would be taken into account.

Sensing that they had done fairly well, and if they lost a little ground, such as Exermont and Montrebeau Woods, that was all right considering the ground they had taken, the Thirty-fifth did not realize what the First Corps and the First Army thought of them. The corps inspector, Lieutenant Colonel Robert G. Peck, was much in evidence as soon as the Thirty-fifth came out of line. He was asking questions that were sharply critical and showing a considerable choler, and they thought this just demonstrated what a headquarters officer did when he was talking to tired and experienced troops who had not had time to clean up and display the polish that a Regular officer was accustomed to on the parade ground. The division's officers and men as a whole did not comprehend how much was out of order—far more than the lack of saluting and the askew uniforms and poor march discipline that Peck openly was criticizing.

When criticism began to mount it came as a shock, and the men of the Thirty-fifth were deeply resentful. Their inclination was to blame it on the Regular Army. Captain Harry Truman did so, and ever after pointed his finger at the Regulars, when he thought of those initial days out of the line and the criticism that increased thereafter, offered by the West Point Protective Association. In later years, one of the reasons he admired General George C. Marshall so much was that Marshall was a graduate of Virginia Military Institute. If President Truman accepted a West Pointer into his confidence it was because of qualities other than the institution the officer graduated from;

for Truman, West Point was a disadvantage, from which the officer in question had to redeem himself. As president, at one point in his administration Truman had it in mind to abolish West Point, not a bad idea he thought, but of course it was impossible.

Something might have come out of the Thirty-fifth's collapse in line in five days, given all that its troubles could have suggested for the Regular Army to reassess and, on the side of the National Guardsmen, for them to try to understand what had happened in terms of cooperating with the Regulars to make it possible to do better next time. Instead the issue of change, once raised, turned into a leveling of blame on both sides. Argument for a while became intense, with three congressional inquiries, bringing in the army's leadership in the persons of Secretary of War Baker and the army chief of staff, General Peyton C. March. Then the issue cooled and disappeared. The Regular Army, failing of congressional appropriations, as had long been its lot in peacetime, went back to its old ways. It retreated into its smaller world of barracks discipline and parade-ground appearance, back into the cocoon from which it was emerging, so one might have thought, in 1917–1918. In the spring of 1919 the men of the Thirty-fifth came home, celebrated their victory parades, and then got out of their uniforms and returned to peacetime pursuits.

I

For a while event followed event as the controversy heated up. Almost at once it became clear that casualties, dead and wounded, had been heavy. The exact totals were difficult to determine, and months and even years passed before they became fairly clear. The question was whether they were 8,000 or 7,000 or, as the War Department said, less than 6,000.

The War College study of 1921–1922 had an explanation that was probably correct, in regard to the manner in which estimates varied. For one thing, infantry officers estimating their casualties naturally saw that their own men were dropping out, and believed that casualties were high as well in other parts of the division. In the infantry brigades it is apparent that casualties were 50 percent. The two brigades at the outset of the battle numbered 14,000 rifles. To see half of them lost was a shattering experience. There also was, the War College concluded, the problem of stragglers. When the troops came out of the line, all of the missing men were obvious by their absence. By the time the engineers' line was established it had become clear that straggling was everywhere, and it was evident well before that, when Major Kalloch went back into Montrebeau Woods and tried to gather enough men for an attack, in the early morning of September 29. The woods was full of men, but he could not find organized units and in the end managed a bare 120 men in his thin force on the left side of the attack. Opinion differed as to why the men straggled. Generals Liggett and Craig in the First Corps thought it was real straggling, not merely being lost, and instructed General Traub and Colonel Bugge to arrest stragglers. They wanted the names of all officers who reported back late, after the division left its sector.[1] Whatever the reason, straggling was extensive and made a big difference in deciding what casualties were, if counting was done in the first day or two after the division withdrew.

As the stragglers drifted in, the casualty figures tended to go down. By the evening of October 2 the strength of the regiments had increased by one-third. So Bugge reported to the corps inspector two days later. On October 1 the two infantry brigades totaled 5,000, with the strength of the regiments varying. The 137th reported 1,300 present; the 138th, 1,200 present; the 139th, 1,500 present; the 140th, 700 present. By October 7 the division had 18,658 men and 699 officers. Known losses by then were killed and wounded, 4,211 men and 135 officers. This left 1,989 men and 14 officers still carried as missing.

The final tally of casualties was nearly 7,300 with 1,126 killed or died of wounds, 4,877 severely wounded, the balance lightly wounded or suffering from combat fatigue and returned to duty.

The question was whether losses were excessive, and by some measure they were not. A prejudiced witness was General Traub, who in a hearing before the Rules Committee of the House of Representatives said they were not. Traub began by stating the question: "The main criticism, as I understand it, is that the losses in the Thirty-fifth Division were unnecessarily high." The answer according to the Thirty-fifth's commanding general was simple. "Now, gentlemen," he said, "in my opinion, they were marvelously low, and I cannot understand why they were so low." The general resorted to history.

> When Gen. Grant attacked the Confederate works at Cold Harbor he lost 10,000 men within about 10 minutes, and he accomplished nothing. We fought five days and nights, constant fighting, with a loss, as I say, of about 500 killed and 4,350 wounded, the great majority of whom were

slightly wounded and who afterwards by the hundreds came back and re-joined the colors. We penetrated to a depth of 12 1/2 kilometers, and ac-complished the other details I have already given you. So much for the unnecessarily great losses.[2]

The War College study adduced some interesting figures pertaining to the First and Second divisions of the AEF, perhaps more pertinent examples than the one Traub gave. At Soissons the First Division lost in casualties 7,400. The Second in the same battle lost 4,500. The Second a little later at Blanc Mont, to the left of the Argonne forest, with heavy fighting in sup-port of the French, lost 4,900. The War College cited the casualties of the First Division when it followed the Thirty-fifth, and these losses, 7,600, often were used to justify those of the Thirty-fifth.[3] The First was the most battle-wise division in the AEF and was fighting for only slightly more than the same territory—it involved retaking Montrebeau Woods and Exermont and going on to take Hill 240 and Fléville to the northwest. The time was a matter of days immediately after, when the German foe was presumably the same, not stronger or weaker than the units the Thirty-fifth met. If the First took that sort of casualties, higher than those of the criticized Thirty-fifth, did it make sense to disparage the Thirty-fifth (save that it was a National Guard division)?

It does seem unfair to compare the tasks of the Thirty-fifth and the First. By the time the First got into position and sought to go forward, it encoun-tered heavy German opposition, as a result of the failure of the Thirty-fifth to hold Montrebeau Woods.

Officers of the First reported that the Thirty-fifth had left an untidy battle-field, which undoubtedly was true, but it did nothing to raise the morale of the Thirty-fifth. The colonel of the Sixteenth Infantry sent in a report stat-ing that his men lived for four days on food stocks left by the Thirty-fifth. He said the Missouri-Kansas division left quantities of rifles and ammuni-tion of all kinds. Colonel Dodds, of the First's artillery, found abandoned ri-fles and other equipment near Baulny, presumably items left by stragglers who did not wish to be bothered with paraphernalia. Dodds said that a bat-tery of the Thirty-fifth stationed near there had chosen poor ground, which resulted in the killing of eighty-six horses.[4]

As mentioned, Lieutenant Colonel Peck began his investigation just after the departure of the Thirty-fifth from its sector and was everywhere asking questions. Some of his queries he barbed by reference to the National Guard.

Three weeks and more before the conclusion of his report to the corps and First Army headquarters got out, admittedly without his name, his anti-Guard remarks were the talk of the division.

Meanwhile, Brigadier General Thomas B. Dugan arrived as commander of the Seventieth Brigade. Dugan was a Regular and possessed no more sensitivity than General Berry. On his first tour of inspection his "keen sense of military neatness," wrote Kenamore, "was violated by the first soldier he saw. Turning to the colonel accompanying him he asked, 'Why do you allow these men to wear these German souvenirs?' The colonel did not understand and Dugan explained: 'Don't you see these knives they are wearing?'

" 'But, general,' the colonel explained, 'that is the American trench knife of the regular issue.'

"The general passed on silently. He had never seen one."

Dugan, it was observed, received the Distinguished Service Medal for his work in handling the Seventieth Brigade in the Meuse-Argonne.

Dugan compounded his insults. A regimental commander turned in a report showing that the men were suffering sickness from drill and hikes in the mud and rain, and Dugan, then temporarily commanding the division, replied, "The health of the command is secondary."[5]

Brigadier General Drum was a good man as chief of staff of the First Army, but he never was noted for tact, and like Dugan he did his best, which was excellent, to raise the temperature of the division. On October 26, Drum, having read Colonel Peck's report, sent all of Peck's conclusions, numbered and therefore conspicuous in their starkness, to Traub. He quoted them verbatim, and perhaps thought thereby that he had gotten that problem solved, off his desk, which in a narrow sense was true, but it was like dropping a bomb on the very thin morale of the Thirty-fifth Division, then in line at Verdun and seeking uncertainly to congratulate itself, despite its casualties and littered sector and Peck and Dugan, that it had done well in the Meuse-Argonne. Verdun, it should be said, was a grisly place for morale-building. Captain Harry Truman wrote that every day German shells were digging up bones of German attackers and French defenders. "There are Frenchmen buried in my front yard and Huns in the back yard and both litter up the landscape as far as you can see. Every time a Boche shell hits in a field over west of here it digs up a piece of someone. It is well I'm not troubled by spooks."[6]

At this juncture Drum's message arrived, with instruction to Traub to disseminate it widely. Its points deserve quotation in full:

1st: That the Thirty-fifth Division at the commencement of operations, September 26th, was not well trained and fit for battle, was not a well disciplined combat unit, and that many officers with the Division were not well trained leaders.

2nd: That the Division Staff was not efficient or well organized.

3rd: That the changes in the Staff and brigade and regimental commanders greatly handicapped the Division Commander in the proper functioning of his Division.

4th: That after the attack started there was no system of liaison. Even the runners failed to follow the axis of liaison prescribed.

5th: That brigade and regimental commanders failed to make use of the means of liaison at their disposal and failed to keep in touch with their higher commanders.

6th: That the failure of all commanders to keep a headquarters established where communications could be received was inexcusable.

7th: That the action of brigade and regimental commanders in going far to the front and out of all communication resulted in their having no more effect on the action than so many company or platoon commanders, and prevented the headquarters in rear from sending orders to units in front.

8th: That if commanders had remained in their headquarters or made provisions for messages reaching them immediately, they would have been able to have had a fair knowledge of conditions, and perhaps have straightened out the many difficulties.

9th: That the intermingling, confusion and straggling which commenced shortly after H hour showed poor discipline, lack of leadership, and probably poor preparation.

10th: That it was a serious error for both the Division commander and the C of S to leave their headquarters at the same time.

11th: That the five attacks which the Division made followed each other so closely that there was no opportunity after the evening of Sept. 26th to reorganize, and get the various units in hand.

12th: That after Sept. 27th the Division was really one in name only as maneuvering power with intact units, except the Engineers, ceased to exist.

13th: That the casualties among the officers was undoubtedly responsible for a great deal of the disorganization.

14th: That most of the straggling and confusion was caused by men getting lost and not having leaders, and not from any deliberate design to go to the rear in order to avoid further fighting.

15th: That the fighting spirit and bravery of officers and men was excellent.

16th: That the failure to have telephone and wireless communication forward to include regiments, and the failure to use the proper code call to

Corps Hqs was due to the inefficiency of Lt. Col. George A. Wieczorek, Signal Corps, then Division Signal Officer.

17th: That the Artillery Commander, Brig. Gen. L. G. Berry, failed to cooperate with and make full use of the Air Service until ordered to do so.[7]

One might well ask whether Drum sent this jeremiad, written by Colonel Peck but going out over his own name, on his own, without consulting Pershing. This seems entirely possible, as his procedure as First Army chief of staff was to send out messages over General Pershing's name. Pershing was more than busy as commander in chief at Chaumont and in addition as the go-between with the War Department, Secretary Baker, and particularly with General March in Washington. Drum's letter does not appear to have had any connection with the new commander of the First Army, Liggett, who had taken over a week or so earlier and was busy with rearranging the divisions for a new attack, the last, on November 1. Liggett had been promoted to lieutenant general, along with Major General Robert L. Bullard, who took over a much smaller group of divisions to the east of the Meuse that was denominated as the Second Army with the mission of preparing an attack on Metz, scheduled for November 14.

Drum stated at the outset of his letter that the purpose of the document was to ensure that the Thirty-fifth had proper training. This is difficult to believe. If training was the goal, he could have accomplished his purpose with a quiet memorandum personally to General Traub, allowing Traub to take responsibility if the directive for training appeared to criticize the previous training of the division.

Instead the report appears to have reflected the irritation of the First Corps, of the First Army headquarters, and behind it of General Headquarters and Pershing himself, that the Thirty-fifth had done so badly. Pershing could be ever so diplomatic in relieving wayward division and corps commanders. There was a snappish side to his personality, and a certain simplicity in the way in which he liked to get things off his mind.

In transmitting the letter to his officers on October 30, Traub was virtually forced to agree with its findings, even though some of them were critical of him.[8] This may, of course, have made his agreement seem less sharp than it otherwise would have been, but it was a peculiar way of softening a sharp letter. If he had possessed backbone, which it does not appear he did, he would have taken the letter personally to Drum or Liggett or perhaps even Pershing and told one or all that he could not give out such an excoriation—or that he desired to be relieved. Instead he transmitted the criticism with his entire agreement: "That this division was not well trained and fit for battle, was not a well-disciplined combat unit, and that many officers were not well-trained leaders are very true statements." He admitted that for months the division had not had opportunity to train, that in passing out of its sector with the French to the Meuse-Argonne it had spent its time in marching at night, bivouacking in daytime to prevent enemy observation. He related that the division was occupying a new sector, Verdun. And he said that everyone should make the effort of his life "that the country expects of each and every one of us" to use "the wonderful personnel in our ranks" to do the bidding of the commander in chief, American Expeditionary Forces, France.[9]

What with the division's high casualties, the reports from the First Division that the Thirty-fifth had left an untidy battlefield, the visible presence among the men of Colonel Peck asking impertinent questions and making remarks about the National Guard, the appearance of General Dugan, and then the extraordinarily explicit criticisms by Peck that Drum sent to Traub and the latter's acceptance of everything Drum said, the scene was set for trouble, and it quickly came.

Regular Army officers—and the onetime commander of the Thirty-fifth, General Wright, was among them—chose to believe that the ambition of a few men, entirely political, lay at the source of the ensuing uproar over criticism of the Thirty-fifth. These men were field artillery officers, Major Bennett Champ Clark; Major Davis, who was adjutant of the Sixty-ninth Brigade; Colonel Ristine; General Martin, whom Traub relieved just before the battle; and the divisional YMCA man, Henry Allen. Most of the criticism from the Regulars focused on Allen.[10]

It should have been clear to the Regulars, but it was not, that none of these men was critical of the Thirty-fifth because of some advantage, never defined, they might have gained in politics. Bennett Clark was the son of James Beauchamp (Champ) Clark, a longtime member of the House of Representatives, the speaker of the House in 1912, and a near victor at the Democratic national convention that year for nomination for president; for many votes he seemed to be winning, until the convention turned to a dark horse, Governor Wilson of New Jersey. His son naturally had political instincts. Bennett Clark was quick-witted, and perhaps a bit lazy, but his wits made up for his indolence. As the years passed he resorted to alcohol, but that stimulant seems not to have been evident in 1917–1918. In the 1920s he filled out physically, possessing a full face that became fuller. In Missouri he would be known as a stump speaker par excellence, which in the state was a first-class recommendation. Before the Thirty-fifth went into action he left the division. He became a U.S. senator in 1933 and was reelected. But this likely suspect, in the eyes of the Regulars, does not appear to have been a plotter against them in 1918–1919. His papers in the State Historical Society of Missouri show that he was one of the founders of the American Legion, when a group of officers and men met in Paris after the Armistice and established one of the two most successful veterans groups in American history, the other being the Grand Army of the Republic. There is no evidence that Bennett Clark, busy with the legion, gave much attention to the Thirty-fifth Division's problems.

Dwight Davis became secretary of war in the administration of President Calvin Coolidge and, perhaps more to his enduring fame, was the donor of the Davis Cup in tennis, but beyond those achievements he held no political ambition at that time. A suave man, born to wealth, he had achieved his prowess in tennis at Harvard, where he was a national champion in doubles. A lawyer thereafter, he did not practice but espoused worthy causes. He obviously was a man with a future and concerned the Regulars. In 1918 his photograph shows him fitting well into the military, with a Pershing mustache and searching eyes, gazing calmly away from the Signal Corps photographer. His work in the division was as an adjutant, the assistant to General McClure, who was a Regular, dismissed by Traub. McClure's successor, Nuttman, was another Regular. There could have been no scheming with them, and if he did any elsewhere it has not come to light.

Colonel Ristine was an independent-minded officer who after the war sided with Martin against Traub. Although General Wright believed he was planning to run for governor of Missouri, there is no evidence that was the case.

Nor was General Martin behind everything that the Regular Army might have feared. He was a calm, careful, honest man who had gone into the Guard because he believed in military preparedness. He had been in the Philippines during the insurrection and displayed bravery in that place where American soldiers constantly were in danger of ambush and sudden death. Thereafter a teacher, then a lawyer (he and his wife both attended the law school at the University of Kansas), he practiced in Fort Scott, Kansas. But his attention turned back to Guard affairs, which he gave ever more time.

From 1909 to 1917 he had been adjutant general of Kansas, the highest Guard officer in the state, and he resumed the post within days after returning to Kansas, upon reappointment by Governor Allen. He was present on the pier in New York harbor when the Thirty-fifth returned from France; Allen sent $3,000 to cover the reception of the Kansas soldiers.[11] Martin in 1920 was president of the national adjutants general association. That year he campaigned among the adjutants general for appointment as the Guard's representative to the War Department's militia bureau, a position that carried the rank of major general, but he lost to Colonel George C. Rickords of Pennsylvania. This ambition had no discernible political purpose, his only goal to be at the center of relations between state Guard officers and the Regulars in Washington. To be sure, he was irritated, angry, and as he wrote his wife humiliated over the manner of his relief just before September 26, and should have been. At first he did not understand why Traub relieved him, and in fact never did, except in terms of Traub's offhandedness and hostility to Guard officers with such a background as he, Martin, possessed. Because of censorship until the war was over he wrote his wife cautiously, but she read between the lines and at once got into communication with his successor as state adjutant general, Brigadier General H. W. Clark. Martin worked with his friend Governor Allen to obtain hearings before congressional committees and went to Washington to testify to the Senate Military Affairs Committee. His papers in the Kansas State Historical Society show nothing more than this activity.

Governor Allen was a longtime Kansas Progressive and a close friend of the publisher of the *Emporia Gazette,* William Allen White. Like White, he was a supporter of Theodore Roosevelt. Born in Pennsylvania, he had "gone West" and was twice elected governor. He served briefly in 1929–1930 as U.S. senator, when Charles Curtis resigned to take office as vice president in the administration of President Herbert Hoover. When the issue of the Thirty-fifth versus the Regulars arose in 1918, he already had been elected governor. He had been present in the Meuse-Argonne and observed what mismanagement could do to a big division composed of ten thousand Kansans who were writing letters to the newspapers and appealing to him as governor.

The Regulars naturally saw Allen as a troublemaker, which he was entirely capable of being. A small, portly, bald man with a domed forehead and arched nose, he was an excellent platform speaker. He knew how to engage an audience. But the conferral of political ambition upon Allen was unfair, for it was unrealistic to think that upon return home to be governor he was not supposed to say anything about what he had seen. He of course read the newspaper accounts and the letters sent to him. He himself was incensed and wanted to do something, and as governor he was in a position to make himself heard.

Inaugurated in January 1919, the governor of Kansas immediately after the inaugural ceremonies met with a group of relatives and next of kin of Thirty-fifth Division soldiers and talked to them at length about what he had seen as division secretary of the YMCA. He told about the wounded, how they lay out where they had fallen for a day or two, until picked up and taken back. He spoke of the lack of artillery support, how after the first day the American artillery was conspicuous by its absence, meaning that it was a case of infantry against enemy machine guns and artillery. He explained that, while the Thirty-fifth advanced for a while, the casualties were far more than they should have been, if the men had had artillery support. This raised the issue of air support, which he said was almost nonexistent. It was bad enough to have had enemy planes raking the lines with their machine guns, but it was far worse to have had them hovering over the lines spotting for German artillery. He said German planes came and went at will. Food was continually a problem for front-line troops, and he mentioned how the rolling kitchens did not get up for four days. He said that the men received two-pound cans of bully beef, with four men assigned to a can, with the result that whenever a soldier carrying a can was separated from his buddies he would open the can, eat what he wished, and throw the rest away. He remarked how the men, clad in summer uniforms and underwear and without overcoats or blankets, were sent up into the Meuse-Argonne where the weather was cold and it rained virtually all the time after the first day.

The relatives and next of kin of Thirty-fifth Division men evidently received the governor's talk with distress. It was published in the Kansas and Missouri newspapers and brought a stream of mail from wounded soldiers and officers sent home early—the division itself did not come home until April. Some officers had gotten home early and were discharged, such as a physician, the division's psychiatrist, resident in Chicago, and he wrote the governor in outrage over how the wounded had suffered, as he was head of the triage at Cheppy and on the scene. The governor later testified that he received one hundred letters, every one of them supporting his critical view of management of the division.

Increasing the clamor that something needed to be done was the publication of the field messages of Ralph Truman, the 140th's intelligence officer. Truman wrote vividly and omitted nothing. It was by chance that his messages got out. He sent them home to his wife, doubtless certifying that his letters contained nothing not passable by the AEF censor. His wife received the messages, did not know what they meant, and thought they were a history of the battle. A friend who had been with Truman when the latter was in the Philippine Islands helping suppress the insurrection, and was a reporter for the *Kansas City Star,* asked Mrs. Truman if he might see the messages, and she gave them to him. Soon they were in the newspaper, graphically showing the division in straits, including the story of the formation of the engineers' line. Governor Allen saw that they showed how tenuous was the Thirty-fifth's condition, specifically that of the 140th Infantry, the only regiment that stayed together, and how Captain Truman was appealing vainly for help.[12]

2

Allen got in touch with the Kansas delegation to Congress, both the representatives and the senators, and the result was a resolution laid before the House of Representatives by his friend and supporter Representative Philip P. Campbell asking for a congressional investigation. There followed three sets of hearings. One was by the House Rules Committee, of which Campbell was a member. The second was by the Senate Committee on Military Affairs. A third, which did not address directly the issues that Allen raised but supported them, was a hearing before the Senate Military Affairs Committee on the Army Appropriation Bill of 1920 in which the committee heard Brigadier General Martin, who testified in his role as adjutant general of Kansas; the committee inquired as to his relief just before the battle, and Martin frankly obliged. In the House hearings the witnesses were Secretary of War Baker, General March, Allen, and General Traub. The Senate committee heard Allen, Traub, and, on the appropriation bill, Martin.

It is clear that the uproar in Missouri and Kansas created by Allen's talk to the friends and relatives of the men and officers moved Secretary of War Baker to damage control. The last thing he desired from Congress was a formal investigation, as had happened after the Civil War. He appears to have made a special plea to the Rules Committee to come before it almost at once. He and General March appeared on January 24. There were no more hearings, House or Senate, until nearly a month later, February 17.

Secretary Baker had a large reputation for being quick to contain criticism.

He spoke rapidly, and what he said was nicely put. A lawyer, as well as a former mayor of Cleveland, he raised technical questions with the committee. To determine what had happened to the Thirty-fifth Division, he said, it would be necessary to have the AEF's commander in chief present, as well as the corps commander. Many officers had not yet returned. The records were not easily available. Complaints had been raised about artillery protection for the Thirty-fifth, contending that the division had little such protection and in some attacks none. He said it would be necessary in regard to artillery support to get information from army and corps artillery commanders. He looked forward to a general inquiry over the conduct of the AEF, as after the Civil War. He was a student of the earlier war and liked to make comparisons, as everyone knew. But a general inquiry was a large undertaking. After the discussion about artillery support he said the same problems would arise with an investigation into other problems.

The secretary stressed the nature of battle in the Meuse-Argonne. "Of course, Mr. Chairman, may I say this? The action in the Argonne forest was the most difficult military enterprise ever undertaken by anybody. The A.E.F. was not merely advancing over no-man's-land but attacking the so-called Hindenburg or ultimate line of defense of the German Army, and the operations there were certainly larger than they were in the St. Mihiel fight, for instance, or in every other engagement in which the Americans participated." In truth, Baker did not know much about military affairs, and his testimony to the committee, apart from being glib and general in nature, displayed that fact. He knew a good deal less than he should have. "May I ask whether or not it is the intention of the war department," Representative Campbell inquired of him, "to bring back the members of the 35th Division officers and men within a reasonably short time?" It was not much of a question. Nor was the answer he received much of an answer: "I will let General March answer that, because I do not remember just what brigade [sic] that is."[13]

Baker was a cipher within the War Department, although the committee members did not know that. March had relegated him to those decisions involving conscientious objectors, social conditions surrounding military installations in the United States, and general military issues that arose in the president's meetings of the cabinet. At the outset of March's tenure in the War Department an incident occurred that demonstrated his relations with the secretary. The two had adjoining rooms, and in the tenure of March's predecessors, Hugh L. Scott and Tasker H. Bliss, a wire had been installed with a buzzer, by which the secretary could buzz for the chief of staff. The first time he was buzzed, March went into the secretary's room. He realized what had happened and upon leaving Baker's office had the wire pulled out of the wall.

The secretary of war and army chief of staff did their best, which was not altogether effective, to prevent an investigation—their efforts were effective in that there never was an investigation, only hearings, but their points were not well made. They sought to refute Allen's charges one by one. In regard to the wounded they said the army was doing its best in an unprecedented situation. March said there always was artillery support for the troops, corps and army artillery, and this remark seems to have inspired more letters to Governor Allen relating that the general did not know what he was talking about. Air support, Baker and March said, was there, if not always on the appearance of German planes. Food always was a problem on a battlefield. Clothing too, but the army was doing its best.

On specific points the secretary and general sought to fill in the House committee. Someone asked March about the relief of Generals McClure and Martin. His answer was surprising. "The element of personal leadership does not play any part any more in a modern fight."[14] He may have been referring to General Pershing or other individuals in the AEF who had spoken critically of him and the War Department. More probably he was saying that leadership in battle, so evident in the Civil War, was impossible on a modern battlefield. He could not have meant that responsibility could have no origin.

Governor Allen appeared almost a month later, and he did exceedingly well. He had had a long experience in politics and in speaking and knew how to deal with committees. No one could have done any better. Both with the Rules Committee of the House and the Military Affairs Committee of the Senate he stayed on the subject and upon interruptions—some of them in the House committee were garrulous, those in the Senate usually to the point—he answered well and resumed his orderly exposition. He could be playful on occasion, which helped with both committees, more so with the House, where his auditors did not seem much interested in what he had to say, save for Representative Campbell. In the House hearings the chairman, Edward W. Pou of North Carolina, was of little help to the governor in keeping order.

Allen was particularly effective on the subject of casualties. He had seen the plight of the wounded and was touched by the attention his address created among the relatives and next of kin. Here he was helped mightily by newspaper stories quoting Dr. Harry R. Hoffman of Chicago. He read Hoffman's description of the Cheppy triage into the record.

> Imagine the plight of our wounded. There were 800 at the advanced dressing station; 1,400 more at the triage, just back of the fighting lines. Some were legless; others armless; many with sides torn out by shrapnel. All, practically, were in direct pain. It was bitter cold. The mud was knee-deep. A half sleet, half rain was beating down mercilessly. And for 36 hours those 2,400 men were compelled to lie there in the mud, unsheltered. We had neither litters on which to lay them, nor blankets to wrap around them.

Hoffman told about the simply awful conditions:

> Noon of September 26, one large tent of the One hundred and thirty-sixth Ambulance Company reached Neuvilly to open triage. Word was received that many wounded were coming. They did not reach us until night of the 26th. It was raining, cold. We could use no lights because the airplanes of the enemy were busy. The wounded came in trucks. There were no ambulances, no litters, no blankets. They were put on the muddy, sloppy ground. Our tent was packed, so many of the men laid outside with no shelter. Hospital personnel took off their coats to cover the wounded, so far as they could.
>
> On the 27th, Maj. W. L. Gist, director of the Sanitary train, consisting of the ambulance companies, sent a runner to Col. [Raymond C.] Turck, the divisional surgeon, saying, "For God's sake send us something—blankets, litters, food." Col. Turck sent back word, "Received your report. Can't do anything; roads blocked."
>
> Gist was going mad. He had 800 men at the dressing stations, with no accommodations. They were out of splints. The chief surgeons had ordered all divisions in the Argonne to use the Thomas hip splints for fractures. All cases were to be splinted where they fell, and external heat was to be applied. They might just as well have ordered a Turkish bath and a Swedish massage. There was no heat and no Thomas splints.[15]

This, to be sure, was no exaggeration. The division was unprepared for thousands of casualties. It had twelve mule ambulances, eight GMC motor ambulances, and three Ford ambulances. An ambulance carried six to eight men. Wounded on the field, if found, were taken to the sides of roads. If fortunate, most of them would be picked up by trucks returning from ammunition runs. The trucks had no springs, and the roads were filled with potholes. Because of the craters below Varennes, the wounded initially could not be gotten out for a day or two. Many did not make it. Below the attack line at Neuvilly some of them were sorted out at a ruined church, which a Signal Corps photographer memorialized in what became a well-known picture, with its roof torn off and the wounded in the aisles and before the altar. To harried doctors along the front the dead were the largest problem, for bodies were difficult to get rid of—it was necessary to dig graves. The living, lying for hours, were classified in the quickest way. Sergeant Triplet spoke to a dentist who was helping and who told him that as one of the walking wounded he, the sergeant, should make his own way to the railroad station and a general hospital, which Triplet managed.

In its detail Allen's testimony on his several subjects was eloquent, far from the political statement-making attributed to him. This was a political leader who went to France as a YMCA representative, a task for which he was unlikely to receive thanks nor, one must guess, votes, for the soldiers could not vote and any advisements they sent home to vote for Allen likely did not arrive until after the election.

The difficulty with his testimony was threefold. For one, he was a civilian, and this stood against him in the eyes of critics who had military experience, had been in action, or thought they had been. For another, he possessed a copy of the Peck report and chose not to use it, beyond citing to a few pieces of information from it.

Allen seems to have believed that he should not take advantage of an army investigative report not available to the public. He did not say anything about this, but it must have been the situation. In his testimony to the Senate committee he related that the report was the single document he took home from France and that he received his copy from the commanding officer of the 137th Regiment. That would have been Major O'Connor, who was a strong Guardsman and was incensed, Allen said (not employing O'Connor's name), by a passage in the report in which Peck blamed the Thirty-fifth's slovenliness on the fact that the Thirty-fifth was a Guard division. It had to have been O'Connor who handed him the copy, which would have been in mimeograph form and available to senior officers. O'Connor was titular commanding officer for a short time until Colonel Hamilton came back into command on the twenty-eighth.

But the point here is that Allen had the report and it was a gold mine of factual detail on the division's collapse—eighty-seven pages of single-spaced typescript, containing the testimony of leading officers as well as statistics taken from official records to which Peck had access. Allen could have used all that material and did not, save for Peck's slurs about the Guard and a table in the report that gave figures on the division's lack of horses. It is possible that the jumbled nature of the testimony and other information in the report was too much for the governor to attempt to master and interpret, and that he therefore did not take advantage of it because of its technicalities, preferring to speak in more general terms. A busy political leader may have had to do that.

The most important difficulty with Allen's testimony, apart from the fact that he was a civilian and his failure to use the Peck report for whatever reasons, was that his testimony moved from subject to subject and was easy to face down in detail. All a hostile witness had to do, and General Traub, on hand for the hearings in both committees, did it, was to take each case and center on it, and if possible make it seem only faintly relevant or even irrelevant.

It is not clear if army authorities sent Traub home specifically so that he could be present for the hearings. He did do good work for the army once he returned. There is a dossier on Traub in the Pershing papers, in the files of general officers and others who got into trouble on the battlefield and elsewhere and were cashiered. When with the Twenty-sixth Division in the winter of 1917–1918, Traub had received a general admonishment from Pershing—at that time he was acting division commander of the Twenty-sixth—and took exception to it, believing its criticism of him personally not fair; Pershing had accused division commanders of making remarks discouraging troop morale and advised them not to do so. The other portion of the dossier in Pershing's papers showed that after the Thirty-fifth came out of the line but before the war was over, the division's grounds during its travels were improperly policed, with the areas where it had encamped being left filthy. Traub may have been removed for that reason—he left the Thirty-fifth on December 29 and went to a depot division, the Forty-first, a skeleton division, with which he went home early in February, well in advance of the Thirty-fifth.

It may be unfair to suggest that Traub as the army's principal representative against Governor Allen was sent into the hearings to redeem his reputation as a division commander. It probably is too much to assume such a purpose on the part of War Department and AEF senior officers. This does not prevent one from thinking that Traub may have considered his testimony a chance to redeem himself. Present in Washington, where the Thirty-fifth was the subject of hearings, he was bound to be asked to testify, and this could be his personal opportunity.[16]

Whatever lay behind his testimony, there can be little doubt that General Traub was a good arguer and point maker and in every particular produced a case for the army that must have pleased the War Department. He was quick-witted and joshed the committee when necessary. All the while he said, repeatedly, that he was commander of the division, knew his job, and understood details of military life. He was a military man. He knew what was possible at the moment, he said, as compared with Allen, who did not see the real actions involving the troops.

Traub said, in regard to the wounded, that "every commander's very first care is for his wounded men, and I assure you that in the A.E.F. the wounded and the sick absolutely received the first and highest consideration, and the greatest care that was at all possible under the difficult circumstances." In a great battle "you cannot provide for every contingency."[17]

After the general made part of his statement to the House committee the questions began. Committee members brought up the complaints of the men. One after another he gave excuses. As for the lack of hot food, he said they could not bring up rolling kitchens and could not cook in daylight. All commanders had easy access to food in nearby dumps but chose not to expose carrying parties to fire. He did not say much about the lack of horses, except that veterinarians examined and passed or rejected every one and that there was no purchasing of nags or gassed horses rejected by the French Army, as Governor Allen claimed. Allen had used a statistic from the Peck report, that the division was lacking 2,702 horses. Traub said the figure (one would have thought Peck had the right figure) was half that, 1,349.[18]

The House committee asked Traub why the men were in summer clothing, and he explained at length that the weather in the Vosges was beautiful and the men did not desire winter clothing. Then when the requisition was made, the material went to a railhead, but the division had moved, and it went to another railhead. When the Meuse campaign began the weather was fine. His explanation did not answer all questions but seemed to. The men were supposed to have a change of underclothing in their packs. They left the packs behind when the division went into battle, "but we got these things up to the men afterwards." "You had on summer underclothing yourself?" asked Representative Campbell. "Yes, sir," was the answer.[19]

There was braggadocio in Traub's testimony, which does not appear to have hurt his case. He told the House committee that on one occasion on the twenty-ninth he had been up at the front at the edge of Montrebeau Woods wearing his binoculars and gas mask and trench coat and carrying his walking (swagger) stick and may have been recognized as an officer of rank. In any event the Germans paid him special attention. Unbelievably, at least to auditors of experience, he said that the enemy had thrown three hundred shells at him, one after the other. His description of his predicament was piquant. He said he zigzagged to throw off the aim of the artillery. They were double-bracketing him—that is, they were throwing two shells to one side to be sure of their aim, then two to the other side, then the fifth shell in the middle, which presumably would have taken him out, had he not been zigzagging. Having caught the attention of his auditors, he remarked that he had made a large mistake at that juncture, which was to assume that the Germans (usually the case, he said) were stupid, but at that point they resorted to single brackets and nearly killed him. At one point a shell struck two and one-half feet from him but failed to explode, the only one in the three hundred that was a dud. All the while a German plane was machine-gunning him, but the bullets fell harmlessly in the wet ground.[20]

As mentioned, the Senate Military Affairs Committee held a hearing over the Army Appropriation Bill of 1920, and General Martin testified. In the course of the hearing he described his taut relations with Traub. Martin knew a good deal about what had happened with the Thirty-fifth but was in a difficult position, since he had been sent off just before the division went into action. He might have told anyway what he had heard, but loyal to his sense of officership, perhaps that one does not speak from hearsay or from confidences, he did not. This fact itself might have informed the army leadership at home and abroad that Martin was no cause of the animosity in the Thirty-fifth against the Regular Army and against what the Regulars described to themselves as a commonsense need for discipline, saluting being an example, generally the evidence of the respect by a soldier toward his officers that made men into good soldiers.

It is of interest that Martin appears to have been in touch with a Regular officer, Colonel Conrad H. Lanza, who was something of a maverick within the Regular establishment. Lanza was an expert on the subject of artillery and a real student in that regard. During the Meuse-Argonne he had been chief of operations for the First Army artillery. After the war he went back to the battlefield and to other places and took photographs and sought to measure the effectiveness of American and German artillery. He gave special attention to the Thirty-fifth Division and from official sources and his own field notes put together a remarkably critical account of how the Thirty-fifth failed, under the title of "The Thirty-fifth Division on September 29th, 1918." In it he remarked the incompetence of General Berry and inferentially of General Traub. A copy of the account is in the files of the Kansas State Historical Society, without evidence of the donor, and must have come from General Martin. How much the doughty Kansas adjutant general learned from Lanza in the early winter of 1918–1919, when Martin was in touch with Governor Allen, or how much he told Lanza, is difficult to say. Certainly, Lanza would have asked his listener or informant to be careful, for Lanza still was in the army.

After the congressional hearings two histories of the Thirty-fifth Division appeared, both in that same year, 1919. One was by Kenamore: *From Vauquois Hill to Exermont.* The other was by Charles B. Hoyt, entitled *Heroes of the Argonne: An Authentic History of the Thirty-Fifth Division.* Kenamore's was the better book. A reporter for the *St. Louis Post-Dispatch,* he wrote well. He opened with a heart-wrenching account of two men, an officer and a sergeant, marooned under a culvert in Exermont when Delaplane and Rieger and their men were forced to retreat. One of the men died. The other was captured by the Germans and lost a leg to gangrene, which set in while he was attempting to stave off capture. The Hoyt book was not as detailed as that by Kenamore, and perhaps not as well written. Both were tributes to the qualities of the men of the division.

Both books harshly criticized the division's Regular Army commanders, with a few exceptions, such as Delaplane. They celebrated National Guard virtues. Hoyt's book concentrated on the Kansas contingent in the division, although published in Kansas City, Missouri. Kenamore sought to deal with both Missouri and Kansas men. Colonel Ristine was an informant of Kenamore, who included a detailed account of Ristine's passage through the German lines—a risky business indeed, for part of the time the colonel was wearing a German helmet and overcoat—that could only have come from the colonel. Ristine was, as mentioned, a partisan of General Martin, provided Martin with all the support he could, and understandably was hostile to the Regular Army.

The books were admirable productions, both readable. Kenamore was outright in criticizing the Regular Army. "The British say," he wrote, "that the battle of Waterloo was won on the cricket lawns of Eton and Harrow. The Thirty-fifth Division had lost its punch on the dancing floors of West Point, in the Efficiency Board rooms at Camp Doniphan, and in the United

States Army system which replaces National Guard officers, however competent, with Regular Army officers, however incompetent."²¹ Hoyt was even more critical.

The books do not seem to have stirred much debate. It is difficult to know how well they sold, or what reviews were like. Their publishing houses are long out of business and records presumably destroyed.

One final attempt to criticize the Thirty-fifth was made privately by its antagonist of October 1918, General Drum. The attempt showed that at the highest command level of the AEF, namely, with General Pershing, there was sensitivity to the issues raised by the Thirty-fifth's collapse. Pershing, it is clear, wanted the issues to die—however much his hand may have been in Drum's critical letter passed to General Traub in the war's last weeks.

After the war the Regular general officers usually dropped down in rank, and Drum went down to colonel—not much of a drop, considering that he entered the war as a captain. He was stationed at Fort Leavenworth. George Marshall, having dropped to captain and then risen to major, was at this time Pershing's aide, and his task was to put together an official report of the First Army. Because the report would set out details of the Meuse-Argonne, it was a sensitive document. Pershing appears to have left the writing to Marshall, who queried Drum about the failure of divisions in the battle. Drum bridled and wrote Marshall that he wanted the failed divisions mentioned by name.

Drum was in a delicate position, for nominally he was dealing only with Marshall, who had been a colonel when he, Drum, was brigadier general and chief of staff of the First Army, occasionally issuing orders by himself and, until Pershing's elevation to army commander, representing Pershing to all corps commanders and division commanders. Behind Marshall now— it was a twist in representation—was Pershing; when Drum wrote to Marshall he was writing the commander in chief. He nonetheless made his points with the same dispatch he had shown when he gave Traub seventeen points for retraining the Thirty-fifth Division. What he wanted was for the First Army report to name names, to be specific as to what divisions failed. "As to the real facts in the case you know as well as I do that our advance was halted on September 26th due to the disorganization existing in the 35th, 37th, and 79th Divisions." There had been much anxiety, he wrote, as to supplies, road congestion, and other details; investigation had shown ("on my part," he said) conclusively that the anxiety was not justified. The need was frankness. "If a statement similar to what I have made is not included in the report of the First Army, the general public and the military readers must accept the French statements of our inefficiency in this connection." Here he was alluding to the accusation made in General Henri Philippe Pétain's headquarters by staff officers, which an American colonel stationed there who was fluent in French, Paul H. Clark, sent directly to the commander in chief, sometimes in daily dispatches. Premier Georges Clemenceau had been trapped in a traffic jam at St. Mihiel and in fury sought Pershing's relief. This was a sensitive point with the commander in chief, and Drum was making the most of it. He added in his letter to Marshall, almost as a sting: "I feel certain that General Pershing does not desire to avoid the issue in this case." Not merely Pershing would suffer by omission of blame for the guilty divisions but so would veterans of the staff—like Drum.

The contest with Marshall over a final draft for the report on the First Army went on, as is evident in the drafts that came to Drum, which he annotated and sent back, keeping copies in his papers. On February 14, 1920, he was after Marshall again, putting the case somewhat differently. In regard to inclusion of "the actual conditions" that forced withdrawal of the offending divisions, he said that the report "as it now stands passes over the foregoing like a scared rabbit."22

It is difficult to avoid the impression that Pershing was the scared rabbit. He knew the sensitivity of the Thirty-fifth to criticism and would have no more of it. For a short time in 1920, Pershing was a dark-horse candidate for the Republican nomination for president, until another candidate, Senator Warren G. Harding of Ohio, loomed. The Regulars had seen political maneuvering in the Thirty-fifth's criticism of conditions in the division. It is possible that Pershing was not averse to some political maneuvering of his own.

Six

Conclusion

The criticism of the Thirty-fifth Division's handling in the Meuse-Argonne promised a great deal in terms of changing the ways of the Regular establishment, making the country more ready to engage in war if such a course should again become necessary. Before World War I, and in particular in 1914–1917 when President Wilson was seeking both to keep the country out of war and to influence the European belligerents either to stop fighting or at the least to make the war more humane, the weakness of the American army did not help the country's diplomacy. Wilson could obtain attention when he sent cables of protest, and when his personal envoy, his friend Colonel Edward M. House, went to Europe and talked with officials in chancelleries and foreign offices. But the attention was more respectful than serious, for the belligerents, especially the Germans, knew that the American army was seventeenth in size among the world's armies, smaller than that of Portugal. In the first weeks of 1917 when the German government began what was described as unrestricted submarine warfare, its submarines giving no attention to neutral flags on merchant or passenger ships, a Berlin official, knowing that the United States had placed itself in a corner in its demands that Germany respect neutral rights, and therefore might have to join the war on the side of the Allies, remarked that the result of American entry into the war would be "zero, zero, zero." If the United States in 1917 had had a large, well-equipped, and tactically efficient army it is entirely possible that President Wilson's diplomacy could have brought a peace without victory, which was what he and the nation desired.

Unfortunately, the collapse of the Missouri-Kansas division in five days and all that collapse symbolized—the eagerness of the National Guard to do what was necessary to defend the country, Regular incompetence in training the division, the querulousness of the men when they did not do well in the line, the Regulars' turning in upon themselves rather than heeding civilian criticism—did not result in anything more than hearings.

The Regulars did not learn much. General Traub supported by Secretary Baker and General March refuted, to their satisfaction, what Governor Allen was attempting to say. The changes that the army could have instituted were never begun, as it slipped back into peacetime routines. The prosperity of the Harding and Coolidge years, followed by the Great Depression of the 1930s, distracted the officers, including the younger men who stayed in the army hoping for better days. For a while they kept up their interest in artillery and machine guns, inspired by the war, and then mostly gave up. They did not give the attention they should have to the new arms, the tanks and planes. World War II taught its lessons in cruel ways similar to World War I, with the U.S. Army surprised time after time by the tactics and weapons of Germany and Japan.

The Missouri-Kansas men, what was left of them, came back home in the spring of 1919, after the hearings in Washington had run their course, and possessed one single purpose, which was to get out of the army and return to what they had been doing in civilian life—or, as was true of so many of them, change occupations to what was more attractive. War had shown them, if briefly, the wider world; it had taken them to a high place and tempted them. In that sense the war caught their attention and changed their lives. In a national sense it did not prepare the country for future international trouble.

The administrations in Washington continued to think it was possible to conduct foreign policy without military force to back it up. Beginning in the mid-1930s Congress passed a series of neutrality laws with the purpose of keeping the country out of war. For a while after 1941–1945 the veterans of 1917–1918 were still strong politically and might have taken up their problems of 1917–1918 and done something about them. In 1944 they elected one of their own as vice president of the United States and four years later elected him president in his own right. On January 20, 1949, the men of Battery D,

129th Field Artillery Regiment, walked proudly along both sides of the limousine carrying President Truman from the Capitol down Pennsylvania Avenue to the White House. Their president was no friend of West Point and the Regulars and spent much of his time in office reorganizing the military into a scheme with three subordinate services and a secretary of defense who would hold everything together in cooperation rather than rivalry. The president desired an act of Congress providing for universal military training, requiring it of all young men, a vast extension of the National Guard. The act was politically impossible, and he settled for continuation of a draft, which turned eventually into an all-volunteer force.

After the time of President Truman the men of the Thirty-fifth Division did little more in regard to issues of war and peace. Memories of need, want, being pushed almost beyond endurance, and defeat by German defenders who knew how to use artillery and machine guns were blotted out by the good things or at least the amusing things of army life. It all became a subject for discussions at the American Legion conventions and before and after parades on days of patriotism. The men of the Thirty-fifth who had fought at the Meuse-Argonne went to the annual reunions of the division if they could. They diminished in numbers and eventually were no more.

In 1962, President John F. Kennedy, over the protest of former president Truman, allowed the Thirty-fifth, which had fought well in World War II as a Guard unit, to disband. By that time the veterans of World War I were in their middle and late sixties, many of them beyond that, and memories were markedly beginning to dim. And, anyway, those who had been in the division in the Meuse-Argonne in 1918 had never really understood what had happened to them.

A Contemporary Analysis

Anyone confronting the organization and operations of the American Expeditionary Forces in 1917–1918 must marvel at how quickly everything was done and—especially on November 1, 1918, when the AEF with machine-like efficiency made its final attack in the Meuse-Argonne—how well. Neither the French nor the British armies in their first actions of the war did so well. General Pershing had his limitations, he was not the complete general, but—everything considered—he and his field commanders deserved the plaudits they received.

What concerns the student of American participation in the war is whether matters could have been managed better, and in that regard the answer has to be a resounding yes. There was no reason the Thirty-fifth Division, which in some sense committed all the errors the AEF could have made, had to collapse. Its men, and its many intelligent officers, deserved better.

For this reason it is of much interest to see what Colonel Carl L. Ristine wrote just after the armistice in 1918. He displayed a remarkable understanding of what he had been through and what his regiment, division, and the AEF might have done differently. To the historian, his observations constitute a compendium of military wisdom. To be sure, he possessed the advantage of a few weeks of hindsight. By Regular measurements he was a Guard amateur and a troublemaker. But his analysis was, one might conclude, a sort of model throughtpiece of the sort that Regular officers in the years prior to 1917, with all the advantage of reports from European battlefields that they had at hand, could have produced, had they not been bound by their training and experiences in the Indian wars, the Spanish War, the Philippine insurrection, the occupation of Veracruz, and the expedition into Mexico.[1]

In compliance with memorandum order Headquarters 70th Infantry Brigade, 20th November 1918, I hereby submit a report dealing with the feature of recommendations as set forth in paragraph two, memorandum Headquarters 35th Division, 19th November 1918.

Training of troops

The training schedules have invariably been too long, consisting of intensive training daily for six days in the week, of from seven to ten hours. Training over long periods, namely, any period exceeding ten weeks to three months, results in but one inevitable conclusion—to wit, stale troops. A highly trained, stale organization is not near as efficient in a battle, or any kind of a contest where humans are pitted against each other, as an organization not so highly trained, but full of pep, snap and enthusiasm.

Schools

In my opinion the army has been schooled to death at the expense of cooperation and teamwork. We have always had a great many of our officers and men attending special schools, which kept them away from their organizations, with the result that when they came back they were, or thought they were, highly trained specialists, and too good for ordinary soldiering. The result was that we had no cooperation or teamwork, and an army composed of highly trained specialists lacking cooperation and teamwork is far less efficient than a group of men with a moderate amount of training who have plenty of cooperation and teamwork.

We have too many special units in the regimental organization, and nine times out of ten when you make a specialist out of a man you ruin him as a soldier. In the fight in the Argonne-Meuse region the specialists were practically worthless for several reasons. In the first place, as specialists they had lost the art of being soldiers. In the second place they were armed with special weapons, and no provision had been made for getting those weapons forward as fast as the infantry proceeded forward, and there was no provision made for keeping those special units supplied with ammunition.

Arrangements should be made for accompanying guns to go with the attacking battalions, and the most practical way to get these guns forward would be to have them motorized, with ammunition carried forward by motorized power, with more or less protection from shelling. For instance, tanks could be utilized for hauling artillery forward; and motorized buses, with protection similar to that afforded by the tanks, should be used to haul artillery ammunition forward.

Continuous orders for attacks

Continuous orders for units to attack, issued by the higher commanders when they are ignorant as to the conditions under which the attacking organizations are laboring, will invariably result in disorganization. One of two things should be done: either the higher commanders should keep in close personal touch with the attacking organizations, so that they would know when it was advisable to order attacks, and when it was advisable to give those organizations an opportunity to reorganize; or the commanding officers of the lower organizations and units should be given a wider latitude and discretion in determining as to when an order for attack should be executed. Personally, I would be in favor of giving divisional, brigade and regimental commanders a wider latitude in determining when and how the attack could best be carried on.

Secrecy of operations

There is too much secrecy within the army, corps or division in regard to when and where operations are to be carried on, and the officers who are directly responsible for the success of these operations have not been advised as to what was contemplated in time to give them an opportunity to study the maps and terrain. Considering that there is danger of the enemy obtaining advance information as to a proposed attack; nevertheless, in my opinion, an attack could be carried on far more successfully with officers who have been well advised and well informed as to the contemplated operation, even if the enemy may also be advised of such contemplated operation. If our concentration of men and material is not sufficient to put on a successful operation even if the enemy may have some advance information of the contemplated operation, in my opinion, it is not advisable to attempt such operation.

Operations against machine guns and 77s

Where troops are operating against a defense consisting primarily of machine guns and artillery, in my opinion, practically all of the attacks and movements forward should be made under cover of darkness, using the artillery as a guide to the attacking troops rather than for the purpose of destroying the enemy positions. Machine guns and artillery cannot operate successfully against an advancing army when they cannot see the advance, and it is much easier to locate machine guns when firing at night than when operating in the daytime. Where troops are operating against such a defense, there is practically no danger in shoving the organization through and behind the defensive organizations, because the defensive organizations have not sufficient manpower or troops to cause the offensive organization any trouble, even if they may be in the rear. If troops were operating against strong infantry organizations, then it would not be advisable to push them forward at night, as the troops in the rear might be strong enough to cut off and isolate the attacking troops, and thereby cause them greater losses.

Operations in daytime

Where the infantry is operating against a machine-gun defense as used by the Germans in the Argonne-Meuse operation, the most dangerous thing that the infantry can do is to follow the instructions as laid down by all the pamphlets and circulars which I have seen, namely, the pamphlets and circulars which I have read advised the infantry to lie down whenever they come within heavy machine-gun fire and immediately commence an operation for the purpose of outflanking the machine guns. The troops who attempted this method of reducing the machine-gun position met with disaster for several reasons. First: the machine guns were so distributed that you could not outflank one without running into another, and every time the troops attempted a forward movement, which they thought was a flanking movement, they met with severe losses, and would immediately lie down and attempt a flank movement along some other part of the line. Each one of these movements met with the same result, namely, severe losses, because each group which attempted to go forward found that they were running into more machine guns, and were not actually flanking any of the guns. It was only a matter of a short time until the morale of the troops operating under such adverse conditions was practically gone, and it was almost impossible to get them up, because they soon realized that every time they got up they were subjected to a well-aimed, heavy machine-gun fire. The more successful way of operating against such a defense is to make the movement forward one continuous movement, advancing in thin lines, with the various lines separated with greater distances than those prescribed in the regulations.

Troops should not be ordered forward against such machine-gun positions without some artillery support. The artillery support will not cause much damage to the enemy machine-gun positions, but the mere fact that the attacking troops are supported with their own guns bolsters up the morale and makes it possible for them to continue the advance against heavy fire. The attacking troops should also fire frequently with their own weapons, even though they are unable to locate the machine guns. This frequent firing bolsters the morale of the attacking troops and causes more or less nervousness among the defending troops. While it is practically impossible to locate any particular machine gun where there is a line of, or a group of, machine guns firing at the same time, nevertheless, firing in the general direction of these machine guns will do a great deal of good.

Frequent movements

This division, and I suppose all American divisions, have spent about nine-tenths of their time and energy in moving from one location to another, and during all of this movement they were obliged to carry with them great quantities of ammunition, rations and heavy guns. If the movements could be cut down, a great deal of energy would be saved which could be used up in actual fighting. If it is not possible to cut the movements down, certainly it would be possible to establish large ammunition and supply dumps at various points where operations were contemplated, so that the troops could equip themselves with rations and ammunition just before entering the operation, and would not be obliged to wear themselves, and large transports, out dragging these things all over the country.

The divisions have operated as separate and independent concerns. Each division attempts to monopolize the roads and take every advantage of the other divisions in order to get their particular trains and supplies and artillery to the designated place, with the result that the roads have become congested, and it has been impossible for any of the organizations to accomplish the desired end. When an army is operated it should be operated as an army, and not as fifteen or twenty separate divisions within that army. By this I mean that the individual, or individuals, directing the army should take charge and direct it as one organization, rather than attempting to direct the various divisions as separate organizations. If directed along these lines it would be possible to establish ammunition and supply dumps where the divisions entering the battle could equip themselves just before entering. The artillery of these divisions could be pushed forward with them, and when it became necessary to relieve a division, an exchange of guns, surplus ammunition, food, and other supplies could be effected, and a great deal of road congestion and heavy pulling by animals would be done away with. As conducted in the recent operation, each division was burdened with a great deal of ammunition, food, guns and other supplies, in getting into the fight, and after being relieved they were obliged to bring all this stuff out again; and the incoming division was obliged to drag all of their stuff in the sector. This was caused because there was no cooperation as between divisions. As an illustration—this regiment had a great deal of difficulty in getting ammunition and food forward in the Argonne-Meuse operation, and at the time we were relieved we had twelve or fifteen wagonloads of rations, besides considerable ammunition, but owing to the fact that we were unable to make an exchange with the incoming division, we were obliged to haul this out, and the other division was obliged to haul an equal amount into the sector. This applied likewise to the artillery, machine guns and other units.

It will probably be urged that continuous use of guns would wear them out, but I take it it would be better to wear out some of them and give the infantry and fighting units some real support, than to wear out the animals in attempting to make the exchange of the guns, thereby depriving and lessening the amount of support afforded the infantry.

Reserve rations and ammunition

In the past an attempt has been made to keep all troops supplied at all times with two days' reserve rations, and the belts full of ammunition. Where troops are marching a great deal from place to place, this reserve ration frequently becomes wet and useless, or the men consume them or throw them away in order to lighten their burden, and a great deal of ammunition has been thrown away because it was so heavy to carry and it seemed to the men a useless thing to carry the ammunition day after day when they did not have an opportunity to use it.

It may be urged that a well-disciplined organization would keep this reserve ration and ammunition, and would not waste it or use it unless properly authorized to do so, but I have never seen a division which was sufficiently disciplined to accomplish this purpose. Certainly it would be a great saving of labor and energy if arrangements could be made to relieve the various organizations of the necessity of always carrying this with them.

While troops are in action the divisions on the firing line should be supplied and fed as one large organization rather than as separate divisions, and this should be conducted and be placed in charge of one individual. For instance, during one period the roads should be used exclusively for the purpose of getting food forward to the troops. At another period the roads should be used exclusively for some other purpose. The order of priority depending upon the urgency of the various articles. It frequently happened that adjoining divisions attempted to use the same roads for various purposes, namely, while one division was attempting to get food forward the other divisions were attempting to get their artillery forward on the same roads, with the inevitable result that road congestion practically blocked all organizations and made it impossible for anyone to accomplish the desired end.

Military police

The military police, or some other organization, should be on hand with full knowledge as to the locations of the various organizations, so that they could direct and advise any and all persons as to their respective locations. It frequently happened that the M.P.'s were instructed not to divulge the location of various P.C.'s [posts of command] and organizations, and it more frequently happened that they were totally ignorant about these matters. Troops will always have more or less straggling, and they will always have more or less soldiers who become lost and detached from their organization, and unless there is some well-organized organization to intelligently direct these soldiers as to the location of their units, the strength and fighting efficiency of the combat organizations will dwindle until they become practically negligible.

Retreats

In the recent operation attacks were ordered at a time when the organizations should have been given an opportunity to reorganize, with the result that they went forward and captured ground with heavier losses than they would have sustained if they had been given an opportunity to reorganize, and with the additional result that a withdrawal was ordered and the casualties were greater during the withdrawal than during the advance forward. The advance forward should not have been ordered unless organizations were in a position to hold the ground after same had been captured, as the losses are invariably greater during a withdrawal than during an advance.

Notes

Chapter One. Preparation

1. *American Troops at the Argonne,* hearings before the Committee on Military Affairs, February 22, 1919, U.S. Senate, 65th Cong., 3rd Sess. (Washington, D.C.: Government Printing Office, 1919), 50.

2. The prejudice of Regular Army officers against the National Guard was difficult to avoid. It appeared in subtle ways. A War College study of the Thirty-fifth Division after the war concluded that the term *National Guard* referred not to the quality but to the character of the division. Inspectors from the First Army and from General Headquarters observed the division on the march and in camp in 1918 and all used the term, in criticism, which they said was "natural and convenient." *35th Division: 1917–1918* (Washington, D.C.: War College, 1921–1922), 22. This study was distributed in mimeograph form in fifty numbered copies, several of which are in the library of the U.S. Army Military History Institute, part of the Army War College at Carlisle Barracks, Carlisle, Pennsylvania.

3. "Came the day. D Company of the Border Rats swung into our company street, wheeled into line like the Rockettes, clicked to a halt, and smartly ordered arms with two cracks and a muffled thud. 'Stand at hease.' 'Hat ease.' The two D companies looked each other over with that speculative, inimical curiosity typical of all military units on their first meeting. We couldn't tell how they felt about it but we were impressed. They were obviously veterans. Their white breeches, faded shirts and hat cords, the nonchalance of their precision drill, and the efficient quiet with which they occupied the line of tents across the street proclaimed their long service" (William S. Triplet, *A Youth in the Meuse-Argonne: A Memoir, 1917–1918,* ed. Robert H. Ferrell [Columbia: University of Missouri Press, 2000], 12).

4. The U.S. Navy gathered in force outside the harbor of Santiago, its ships arrayed around the narrow entrance so that when the Spanish squadron chose to come out, each American vessel could "charge." When smoke betrayed the squadron's

intention, and the navy's ships charged, they got in each other's lines of fire and risked collisions.

5. See Ralph E. Weber, ed., *The Final Memoranda: Major General Ralph H. Van Deman, USA Ret., 1865–1952, Father of U.S. Military Intelligence* (Wilmington, Del.: Scholarly Resources, 1988). In these posthumously published memoranda General Van Deman showed how little support there was for intelligence operations in the War Department. Not much happened until after the Civil War and the Indian wars, and little more from the mid-1880s until 1917. At first the concern was the Western Hemisphere, principally Cuba and the Caribbean. Then it was China, but not Europe. In China the army's interest was to acquire maps of the area from Tientsin to Peking, so Americans could get out in cases of personal danger. The war of 1904–1905 did not concern the U.S. Army, in spite of what it might have taught about the use of artillery and machine guns. Van Deman did not mention the Russo-Japanese War, at which Pershing among other observers was present. After that war, concern turned to Japan, resulting in the round-the-world voyage of the Great White Fleet. Its original purpose had been to go from the Atlantic to the Pacific, but newspaper attention persuaded President Theodore Roosevelt to send it around the world. In 1908 a reorganization of the War College virtually closed the military information division.

The eventual turn back to military intelligence was a curious business that Van Deman had to maneuver. He had argued with General Scott over establishment of a military intelligence organization, and Scott forbade him to talk to the secretary of war, Newton D. Baker. He had much the same trouble with Scott's assistant and successor, General Tasker H. Bliss. By chance, Van Deman was talking about the trouble with a well-known woman novelist, who was to see Secretary of War Baker. She became incensed with Van Deman's trouble and told Baker about it. Van Deman also knew the Washington chief of police, who breakfasted with Baker every morning, and the chief told the secretary as well. Baker established an intelligence organization, shortly after the United States entered the war (21–22).

6. See n. 2, above.

7. *35th Division*, 1. The leading student of AEF tactical ideas is James W. Rainey, whose work is basic to the subject. See his "Ambivalent Warfare: The Tactical Doctrine of the AEF in World War I," *Parameters* 13 (1985): 34–46, and "The Questionable Training of the AEF in World War I," *Parameters* 22 (1993): 89–103. But there were more problems than confusing tactical doctrine; for them see Timothy K. Nenninger, "Tactical Dysfunction in the AEF, 1917–1918," *Military Affairs* 51 (1987): 177–181. The author relates personnel policies that led to unsystematic choosing of noncommissioned officers, the relief of officers for attendance at army schools, the crude replacement system, the unwieldy size of divisions, and lack of division "tail"—service troops. Some related to thoughtlessness, others to lack of time in training in the United States and France.

8. *35th Division*, 9.

9. "When I went into one of the brigade mess halls there sat old General Lucien

G. Berry and three Regular Army colonels. General Berry had been the ranking field artillery colonel at the outbreak of the war and had been General Pershing's chief of artillery on his march into Mexico in 1916. He was six feet tall, wore a handlebar mustache and hated National Guard lieutenants. The old man was fond of privates and corporals but took much pleasure in chewing up young officers with his false teeth and spitting them out in small bits—but I'll say this for him, he would not let anyone outside his outfit find fault with his officers or men. Well the general and his three colonels took me over the jumps for about an hour and I came out very sure I'd never be promoted. Then Ted [Marks] went in. It was getting near lunch time by then so they only kept him thirty minutes. We all got promoted. [Newell T.] Paterson's commission was dated April 22, 1918, mine April 23 and Ted's April 24" (*The Autobiography of Harry S. Truman,* ed. Robert H. Ferrell [Columbia: University of Missouri Press, 2002], 43–44).

"I had a regular one yesterday. . . . I think I failed miserably because General Berry was so gruff and discourteous in his questions that I forgot all I ever knew and couldn't answer him. He said, 'eh huh! You don't know, do you? I thought so. You don't know. That'll be all, outside.' He kept me and the two others, Lieutenant Paterson and Lieutenant Marks, standing out in the cold so long that we took a terrific cold and I couldn't get up this morning for reveille" (to Bess Wallace, February 23, 1918, in *Dear Bess: The Letters from Harry to Bess Truman, 1910–1959,* ed. Robert H. Ferrell [Columbia: University of Missouri Press, 1998], 245).

10. Col. Jens Bugge interview, in "Report of Investigation by Lieut. Col. R. G. Peck, Inspector General, First Army Corps: Taken October 15, 1918," box 16, Hugh A. Drum papers, U.S. Army Military History Institute. Hereafter cited as Peck report. Bugge was acting chief of staff of the Thirty-fifth Division.

11. *35th Division,* 3.

12. Ibid.

13. Ibid., 4.

14. Ibid., 8.

15. Ibid., 9.

16. "There were occasional fights between our men and theirs. That did not aid in cementing the entente. A British noncom who was a bit of a wag, heard an excellent wheeze at his own headquarters, and hurried to tell it to the Americans. He found three of them together on a sidewalk in Eu. 'I say you fellows. Did you know the next war is to be fought between the two yellow races? Yes, the Japanese and the Americans. Haw!'—gentle hands bore him away to a hospital" (Clair Kenamore, *From Vauquois Hill to Exermont: A History of the Thirty-Fifth Division of the United States Army* [St. Louis: Guard, 1919], 33).

17. Triplet, *A Youth in the Meuse-Argonne,* 112–22.

18. *Dear Bess,* 269.

19. *35th Division,* 18. For acute comments on the lack of communication within divisions, inability with maps, and failure of liaison with neighboring divisions, all delinquencies of the Thirty-fifth Division, see Timothy K. Nenninger, "Unsys-

tematic as a Mode of Command: Commanders and the Process of Command in the American Expeditionary Forces," *Journal of Military History* 64 (July 2000): 762–65. This article unsparingly analyzes the AEF's command delinquencies.

20. Peck report.

21. Nolan papers, comments on General Pershing's memoirs, U.S. Army Military History Institute, 490–91. When Pershing's memoirs appeared in serial form in newspapers in 1930–1931, prior to publication in book form, Nolan sent comments, and he enlarged on them in a thick bound typescript now in his papers.

22. "We never knew anything about the 35th Division except what was discovered by officers from these Headquarters who went out to the Division to obtain specific information and get it back to me. They apparently had no system of liaison in spite of very detailed explanations and demands made by these Headquarters before they went into action. The one thing they used was the wireless and they used that in open uncoded messages, flatly violating orders issued concerning its use. They used this wireless prior to the beginning of the action and after the action opened, failed to use it except in the unauthorized way stated. There is no doubt about it" (Craig testimony, Peck report).

23. Colonel Wieczorek does not appear to have employed the talents of members of the 110th Field Signal Battalion. According to one officer, First Leiutenant Grover C. Freeman, "While in the Vosges I transformed a field buzzer into a wireless transmitting set by increasing the voltage and adding a spark gap; used with a short insulated antenna and counterpois one man could walk right along and transmit messages back to the regimental station up to a distance of three miles, a very useful article for infantry battalions" (Freeman to chief signal officer, AEF, 314.7, January 8, 1919, "Historical Narrative of Signal Corps Officers," entry 2040, RG 120).

24. "Aviation-correspondence of Air Service with 35th Div.," folder 839, box 3130, GHQ G-3 file, entry 267, RG 120, National Archives, College Park, Maryland. All citations from record groups are to the National Archives. In this letter from Patrick to Brigadier General Leroy Eltinge, the head of the air service listed page after page of the Thirty-fifth's delinquencies in communicating with the service.

25. Kenamore, *From Vauquois Hill to Exermont,* 139–40.

26. The War College study contended that there was enough food up front, but the study's logic was involuted. It admitted shortages and attributed them to disorganization in the front lines, which interfered with distribution. It admitted the absence of rolling kitchens, which prevented use of some of the supplies received. Traub asserted that there was no general shortage. Officers of the division said they always knew where to find rations near at hand, and if they did not obtain them it was because they did not want to incur the losses of bringing them up under fire. The First Division found quantities of Thirty-fifth Division supplies throughout the area, much of them rations. The study concluded, "But we do not know, of course, at what date all this came in" (*35th Division,* 57).

27. Triplet, *A Youth in the Meuse-Argonne,* 160.

28. In the Third Battalion of the 140th Infantry the commander called the company commanders together and gave out maps at 7:00 o'clock on the evening be-

fore the Meuse-Argonne attack. Because of the urgent need to gather equipment, the company commanders had no opportunity to study the maps. Capt. S. O. Mc-Fadden of M Company, 140th Regiment, letter of September 17, 1927, box 227, Thirty-fifth Division, American Battle Monuments Commission file, RG 117.

29. Douglas V. Johnson II and Rolfe E. Hillman Jr., *Soissons: 1918* (College Station: Texas A&M University Press, 1999). See also Conrad S. Babcock memoir, Hoover Institution, Stanford, California.

30. Like all general officers sent to Blois, McClure received an evaluation by his peers, for which see box 8, Pershing papers, entry 22, RG 200.

31. For Martin's testimony see *Army Appropriation Bill, 1920,* hearing before the Committee on Military Affairs, February 20, 1919, U.S. Senate, 65th Cong., 3rd Sess. (Washington, D.C.: Government Printing Office, 1919), 6. The military budget for 1920 became an issue in Congress almost as soon as the armistice ended the war. It was clear that something would have to be done to reorganize the army, and Regular-Guard relations were involved. Martin testified as adjutant general of Kansas.

32. Peck report.

33. *Army Appropriation Bill, 1920,* hearing, February 20, 1919, 6; *American Troops at the Argonne,* hearing, February 22, 1919, 52.

34. Donald D. Hay, "Machine Guns, 35th Division, Meuse-Argonne Operation, Sept. 26–Oct. 1, 1918," *Infantry Journal* 40 (May–June 1933): 205.

35. "1916–18" box 1, Lucien G. Berry papers, U.S. Army Military History Institute.

Chapter Two. Thursday, September 26

1. The Thirty-seventh Division had held a quiet defensive sector. The Ninety-first and Seventy-ninth had never been in the front line prior to their concentration for the Meuse-Argonne.

2. For McNair's after-action report see box 3099, GHQ G-3 file, entry 267, RG 120.

3. Traub did not follow up on the Hotchkiss carts. When the present writer was assisting the late General J. Lawton Collins with his memoirs (*Lightning Joe: An Autobiography* [Baton Rouge: Louisiana State University Press, 1979]), Collins related that when commanding an eight-division corps he called morning conferences of division commanders and issued their orders. But, most important, he said (we were walking across the Mall in Washington, D.C., and he stopped and pointed his finger at me), "the next morning I checked to see if they did it."

4. W. L. Schrantz, "Initial Machine-Gun Barrage, 35th Division, Meuse-Argonne Offensive," *Infantry Journal* 16 (November 1919): 367–71. Schrantz was captain of the 128th Machine Gun Battalion. See also Colonel Donald D. Hay's article, "Machine Guns, 35th Division, Meuse-Argonne Operation, Sept. 26–Oct. 1, 1918," *Infantry Journal* 40 (May–June 1933): 193–206.

5. Operations report, Thirty-fifth Division, October 11, 1918, folder 11, box 3315, entry 270, RG 120.

6. William S. Triplet, *A Youth in the Meuse-Argonne: A Memoir, 1917–1918,* ed. Robert H. Ferrell (Columbia: University of Missouri Press, 2000), 164; Milton B. Sweningsen, "My Four Days under Fire," 5, box 2, Thirty-fifth Division survey, U.S. Army Military History Institute.

7. Norman S. Hall and Sigrid Schultz, "Five Red Days: The True Story of the 35th Division in the Meuse-Argonne Battle," *Liberty* 4, no. 2 (May 14, 1927): 9–14.

8. After-action report by Traub, October 4, 1918, box 459, GHQ G-3 file, entry 267, RG 120.

9. *Losses of Thirty-Fifth Division during the Argonne Battle,* hearings before the Committee on Rules, House of Representatives, February 17, 1919 (Washington, D.C.: Government Printing Office, 1919), 24. "Some of the men did not move to take position as I had directed and I spoke sharply, perhaps somewhat roughly, and it was then that I saw what I consider to be as fine an exhibition of uncalled morale as would ever expect to see. One man was able to raise his head far enough from the ground and turn it toward me to show his wounds, and having reached the limit of his strength again fell forward. Another man with a stomach wound tried to roll over to show me why he was not complying with instructions, while still another man whose leg had been shattered by shell fire roused himself sufficiently to try to indicate why he was not moving. And there were others who were trying to show why they could not move. These men while severely wounded and I believe some of them mortally wounded, did not want anyone to think that they were not ready to obey any orders given if it was physically possible for them to do it. I do not know the names of these men but I believe they were some of the Company 'A' men who had become separated from their company in the fog and had been attached to Regimental Headquarters" (Captain H. F. Lyons to Howland, January 5, 1919, 138th Inf. Hq. Co, 235.33.6, box 15, Thirty-fifth Division historical, entry 1241, RG 120).

10. Martin Blumenson, *The Patton Papers: 1885–1940* (Boston: Houghton Mifflin, 1972), 615–16.

11. Clair Kenamore, *From Vauquois Hill to Exermont: A History of the Thirty-Fifth Division of the United States Army* (St. Louis: Guard, 1919), 131.

12. Triplet, *A Youth in the Meuse-Argonne,* 173.

13. M. M. Small, in *Company "A" Twenty-Third Engineers A.E.F.* (Chicago: Stack, 1920), 71.

14. Ibid.

15. "After waiting two or three hours on the 137th Infantry to continue the advance I took the matter up with the commanding officer of such regiment, to ascertain why our progress had been stopped. The commanding officer of the 137th Infantry told me that his regiment had become terribly mixed and demoralized on account of the attack in the early morning and that in his opinion his troops were unable to advance farther forward" (Lieutenant Colonel Ristine, operations report, Thirty-fifth Division, October 11, 1918, box 3315, entry 270, RG 120).

16. Writing to the major's widow, Chaplain Daniel Lane described what happened: "It was just at 3 o'clock in the afternoon of this first day of the engagement when our beloved Major fell. We were emerging from the valley by the German

cemetery on the Eastern suburbs of Varennes, walking up the narrow gauge railway turning to the right and walking up the forks of the Cheppy-Varennes and Charpentry roads, and mounted to the summit of the opposite hill. There had been a hush unnatural, as we reached the summit overlooking the valley in which these devastated towns lay. It was broken by the storm which burst furiously upon us. I was carrying my Major's Musette bag and was a few steps in advance when the enemy's fire swept the heights. The last picture I have of your dear brave husband is the best. It better reveals the unselfish brave warrior that he was. Thinking not of himself at all he stood fearlessly and wheeled about to order his men to stay below when a bullet hit its mark and he fell pierced through the brain without an instant's pain, save that last thought for the welfare of his men" (Clair Kenamore, *The Story of the 139th Infantry* [St. Louis: World, 1920], 23).

17. Peck report.

18. Undated letter (1929), 137th Regiment, Thirty-fifth Division, American Battle Monuments Commission file, RG 117.

19. Kenamore, *From Vauquois Hill to Exermont*, 139.

Chapter Three. Friday–Saturday, September 27–28

1. *Losses of Thirty-Fifth Division during the Argonne Battle,* hearings before the Committee on Rules, House of Representatives, February 17, 1919 (Washington, D.C.: Government Printing Office, 1919), 40.

2. Peck report.

3. Berry's memory was selective; although his brigade did well that evening, it was not fully up and firing. In the spring of 1919 while on the way to the ship he was interviewed by Colonel Upton Birnie Jr., who asked how much of his brigade was up and firing. The answer by then was all of it, "Two regiments of 75s and one regiment of 155s" (general correspondence, folder 459, box 3099, GHQ G-3 file, entry 267, RG 120).

4. Clair Kenamore reported that at Cheppy on the first day the 138th captured one hundred antitank guns that never had been used (*From Vauquois Hill to Exermont: A History of the Thirty-Fifth Division of the United States Army* [St. Louis: Guard, 1919], 123).

5. William Triplet remembered the advice of a British bayonet instructor at Doniphan, "if he turns 'is back, chyse 'im" (*A Youth in the Meuse-Argonne: A Memoir, 1917–1918,* ed. Robert H. Ferrell [Columbia: University of Missouri Press, 2000], 200). Box 3099, GHQ G-3 file, entry 267, RG 120.

6. Triplet, *A Youth in the Meuse-Argonne,* 168.

7. C. B. Allen, "A True Account of the Kansas City, Kansas Boys in the Argonne," Liberty Memorial, Kansas City, Missouri. Allen wrote that during his passage northward with the company he got into Exermont. This was possible, and if so and if he could have held it, it would have been wonderful, for on the twenty-ninth Exermont proved an impossible place to hold (see Chapter 4).

8. Milton B. Sweningsen, "My Four Days under Fire," 16, box 2, Thirty-fifth Division survey, U.S. Army Military History Institute.

9. Kenamore, *From Vauquois Hill to Exermont*, 181.

10. *Losses of Thirty-Fifth Division during the Argonne Battle,* February 17, 27.

11. Anon., *The Cannoneers Have Hairy Ears: A Diary of the Front Lines* (New York: Sears, 1927), 206–7.

12. Sweningsen, "My Four Days under Fire," 17–19.

13. Kalloch to the adjutant general, Washington, D.C., June 9, 1919, "35th Division," box 16, Drum papers.

14. *Losses of Thirty-Fifth Division during the Argonne Battle,* February 17, 44.

15. William M. Wright, *Meuse-Argonne Diary: A Division Commander in World War I,* ed. Robert H. Ferrell (Columbia: University of Missouri Press, 2004), 79–80.

16. Pierpont L. Stackpole diary, September 26, 1918, George C. Marshall Library, Lexington, Virginia. Courtesy of the editor of *The Papers of George C. Marshall,* Larry I. Bland.

17. Lucien G. Berry file, box 8, Pershing papers, entry 22, RG 200.

18. After the Thirty-fifth came out of the Meuse-Argonne, Colonel Nuttman, commander of the Sixty-ninth Brigade, was promoted to brigadier general. By that time, with the record of the Thirty-fifth Division mired in dispute, with Traub's reputation as well as that of Berry in question, one might have thought that Traub would be careful with his evaluations, for fear that fingers might point to his record. Colonel Nuttman's performance as a brigade commander had not been notable. But Traub savaged him in an evaluation. "As a brigade commander I consider him below the average. He has absolutely no 'punch' and has to be forced into energetic action each time you want anything special done, principally so in battle. He makes no special effort to keep his Chief informed as to conditions in time to make a Chief's punch of much avail." "Confidential Reports on Efficiency of Officers Who Served in A.E.F.," adjutant general records (European Expedition [bulky]), decimal 201.6GE, entry 31, RG 407.

19. Bugge, in Peck report.

20. For General Patrick's letter see above, n. 23 for Chapter 1.

21. The information that follows is from Jacobs's report on the Thirty-fifth Division, October 1, 1918, box 3410, inspector general file, First Army reports, entry 24, RG 120.

22. *History of the First Division during the World War: 1917–1919* (Philadelphia: Winston, 1922), 193.

23. Bugge, in Peck report.

Chapter Four. Sunday, September 29

1. Peck report.

2. Donald D. Hay, "Machine Guns, 35th Division, Meuse-Argonne Operation, Sept. 26–Oct. 1, 1918," *Infantry Journal* 40 (May–June 1933): 200.

3. Joseph N. Rizzi, *Joe's War: Memoirs of a Doughboy*, ed. Richard A. Baumgartner (Huntington, W.Va.: Der Angriff, 1983), 114.

4. Delaplane, in Peck report; also Thirty-fifth Division, box 227, American Battle Monuments Commission file, RG 117. In his letter to the commission of April 21, 1929, Delaplane said he was uncertain who gave the order to the Third Battalion, although Davis had told him it was Hawkins. In 1929 the former commander of the 140th was a lieutenant colonel of infantry (tanks) at the Tank School, Fort George G. Meade, Maryland. Hawkins was a brigadier general at Fort Omaha, Nebraska.

5. Letter of October 2, 1918, Violette Collection of World War I soldiers, Truman State University, Kirksville, Missouri. Courtesy of Elaine M. Doak.

6. William S. Triplet, *A Youth in the Meuse-Argonne: A Memoir, 1917–1918*, ed. Robert H. Ferrell (Columbia: University of Missouri Press, 2000), 29, 210ff.

7. Henry J. Reilly, *Americans All: The Rainbow at War* (Columbus, Ohio: Heer, 1936), 658–59.

8. Parker C. Kalloch Jr. to adjutant general, Washington, D.C., June 9, 1919, "35th Division," box 16, Drum papers.

9. Undated letter (1929), 137th Regiment, Thirty-fifth Division, American Battle Monuments Commission file, RG 117.

10. Rexmond C. Cochrane, *The 1st Division in the Meuse-Argonne, 1–12 October 1918* (Washington, D.C.: U.S. Army Chemical Corps, 1957), 22.

11. Comments on General Pershing's memoirs, 489, Nolan papers, U.S. Army Military History Institute. The division machine-gun officer, Colonel Hay, thought the woods could have been held. "Machine Guns, 35th Division, Meuse-Argonne Operation," 204.

12. Fred L. Lemmon, "The 140th Infantry in the Meuse-Argonne" (Infantry School, Fort Benning Georgia, 1923–1924), 11.

13. Sigrid Schultz, in Norman S. Hall and Schultz, "Five Red Days: The True Story of the 35th Division in the Meuse-Argonne Battle," *Liberty*, 4, no. 2 (May 14, 1927): 14.

14. Clair Kenamore, *From Vauquois Hill to Exermont: A History of the Thirty-Fifth Division of the United States Army* (St. Louis: Guard, 1919), 225.

15. Rizzi, *Joe's War*, ed. Baumgartner, 106.

16. Ibid., 106–7.

17. Peck report.

18. According to the captain, "It being a critical moment, I gathered a few of my NCO's and observers about me and stopped about 300 at the point of the gun" (field message 24, 4:20 p.m., September 29, 1918, to G-2, Thirty-fifth Division). Copies of Captain Truman's messages are in the hearings of the House Rules Committee and the Ralph E. Truman papers at the Harry S. Truman Library, Independence, Missouri. Also Thirty-fifth Division historical, entry 1241, RG 120. "If my memory serves me right," his wife, Olive, wrote, "he said he did shoot one man" ("Military Biography," 43–44, Ralph Truman papers).

19. Kenamore, *From Vauquois Hill to Exermont*, 218.

20. "1916–18," box 1, Lucien G. Berry papers, U.S. Army Military History Institute.

21. Rhodes combined the diary with a memoir that recorded his army service. He reported receiving his academy diploma from a smiling William T. Sherman and seeing at West Point the other figures of the Civil War, Generals Philip Sheridan and U. S. Grant. As a cadet he took part in Grant's funeral procession. He was given the usual assignments and served in the usual places—the Sioux campaign, Spanish-American War, Boxer Rebellion, Philippines, Mexico. Near the end of the Meuse-Argonne he was to command the Forty-second Division, but he missed out when, as he wrote, a political decision in the War Department gave command to Brigadier General Douglas MacArthur, the commander of the division's Eighty-fourth Brigade. Copies of the Rhodes diary-memoir are in the National Archives and the Military History Institute at Carlisle Barracks.

22. In all, the army had about ninety-five heavy guns to support the Thirty-fifth. Because of the army order for the attack on September 29, army artillery was not to fire south of a line running from Dun-sur-Meuse to Bantheville and Landres-et-St. Georges, to avoid hitting the advancing infantry, unless asked for by the corps. The army chief of artillery offered the support to the corps chief, but corps did not ask for it until late on the afternoon of the twenty-ninth. Presumably either Traub or Berry could have asked corps for support. In the event, it is unclear who asked.

Chapter Five. Aftermath

1. Pierpont L. Stackpole diary, October 2, 1918, George C. Marshall Library, Lexington, Virginia.

2. *Losses of Thirty-Fifth Division during the Argonne Battle,* hearings before the Committee on Rules, House of Representatives, February 18, 1919 (Washington, D.C.: Government Printing Office, 1919), 67. Grant's losses at Cold Harbor, June 3, 1864, were 5,600 in a force of 60,000.

3. *35th Division*, 52–53.

4. Folder 459, Thirty-fifth Division, general correspondence, box 3099, GHQ G-3 file, entry 267, RG 120.

5. Clair Kenamore, *From Vauquois Hill to Exermont: A History of the Thirty-Fifth Division of the United States Army* (St. Louis: Guard, 1919), 129, 245–46.

6. Truman to Bess Wallace, November 1, 1918, in *Dear Bess: The Letters from Harry to Bess Truman, 1910–1959,* ed. Robert H. Ferrell (Columbia: University of Missouri Press, 1998), 277–78.

7. Peck report.

8. For the Traub letter see Kenamore, *From Vauquois Hill to Exermont*, 252–53.

9. Ibid., 253.

10. General Wright blamed Ristine, Clark, and Davis. "He believes that the

'Governor Allen' material was warmed up for political purposes and that Governor Allen had come over with that definite purpose in view. General Wright also said that he believes there is a limited political clique or organization in the Division now which will reopen the question of the work of the Division on the return to the United States. He mentioned in this connection Colonel Ristine who, he says, he understands will be a candidate for governor of Missouri, Colonel Clark, who is the son of Mr. Champ Clark and who he understands aspires to run for the House of Representatives, and Major Davis who also has political aspirations" (Colonel Upton Birnie Jr., in folder 459, Thirty-fifth Division general correspondence, box 3099, GHQ G-3 file, entry 267, RG 120).

11. Allen to Martin, April 2, 1919, "Martin, Charles I., 1919," box 14, Henry J. Allen papers, Kansas State Historical Society, Topeka.

12. For Captain Truman's field messages see *Losses of Thirty-Fifth Division during the Argonne Battle,* February 17, 26–30, 52–57, and the Ralph Truman papers. The originals are in Thirty-fifth Division historical, entry 1241, RG 120. Traub was sensitive after the war that he did not quickly receive promotion to brigadier general in the Regular Army—his commissions as brigadier and major general were in the National Army and hence temporary. He kept his rank as major general, but his Regular Army rank was colonel. This became apparent when Ralph Truman wrote to him in 1919 asking if Traub would recommend him for a post in the Missouri Guard. Traub replied that he would be glad to do so but had heard that Truman had released the field messages to the newspapers and hence had been a part of the Thirty-fifth's agitation against the Regulars. Although the general did not say so, he inferred that this agitation, the "odious work" of certain men, had prevented him from becoming a permanent brigadier general. Truman wrote immediately to say that he had had nothing to do with the effort to blame the Regulars for the Thirty-fifth Division's woes, and Traub gave him a recommendation. Truman did not say how or why his wife gave the messages to a reporter. Truman to Traub, May 18, 1919; Traub to Truman, May 22, 1919; Truman to Traub, May 25, 1919; Truman to Traub, March 21, 1922; Traub to Truman, March 23, 1922, Ralph E. Truman papers.

13. *Losses of Thirty-Fifth Division during the Argonne Battle,* January 24, 9. Representative Campbell asked the secretary what corps the Thirty-fifth was in. He replied: "I do not remember which corps [it] was in at that time. They were moving around from one corps to another" (7).

14. Ibid., January 24, 15.

15. Ibid., February 17, 35–36.

16. If Traub had in mind a personal redemption, this may explain his extravagant praise of General Pershing in the hearings: "The way that work has been handled by Gen. Pershing and his staff will be the marvel of civilized nations during all future time. The way he has done his work, the farsightedness, the breadth of view, the scope of his plans, and everything is something that will bear the study of all men, more especially of fighters, for a great many years to come. He has done his work in a most marvelous manner. It is not for me, a junior officer, to either praise

or criticize a senior, but when I consider the magnitude of the undertaking, his great responsibilities, the way he prepared for the training of officers and men, with millions being shoved over to him practically untrained in great part, and who had to be prepared for battle amidst unusual surroundings and to compete with extraordinary conditions, against veterans; that in order to do that he had to have this wonderful staff, and had to inaugurate those wonderful schools and everything had to be thought out, and everything had to be looked forward to and prepared for on an immense scale; when I look back upon all those things accomplished it would seem impossible if it had not been done. He did not prepare to handle a few hundred thousand men, but four or five million men, and that accounts for the great scale upon which everything that was done had to be done over there in the A.E.F." (ibid., February 18, 95).

17. Ibid.

18. Ibid., February 18, 67. The horse issue was serious, for the division—as was true of most AEF divisions—had a great shortage. Traub may have felt it best not to joust with Allen about horses, for Allen was a wit on the subject. "We used these old, worn-out horses of the French, in every activity," the governor said. "Because we were so short, and many of them were horses that had been gassed while in the French army, and been evacuated and taken back to assembling corrals, and they could still walk so we bought them." Allen roused the committee.

> Senator Sutherland: And paid the full market price for a sound horse.
> Mr. Allen: Paid $400 apiece.
> Senator Sutherland: That was about the full market price for a sound horse, was it not?
> Mr. Allen: Yes, that was the Frenchman's idea of what he ought to get for any horse that was still breathing. (*American Troops at the Argonne,* hearing, February 18, 1919, 25)

19. Ibid., February 17, 41.

20. *Losses of Thirty-Fifth Division during the Argonne Battle,* February 20, 89. After the Thirty-fifth came out of the line Traub went to corps headquarters and talked with Liggett in the presence of Stackpole, who recorded the conversation with malice. "Traub rather worn out, but full of talk, primarily with reference to his own experiences when personally visiting brigade commanders in search of information which he says he could not otherwise procure. He lived without sleep for four days and nights, subsisting exclusively on coffee and cigarettes, was the net target of every German battery, and frequently bracketed in the open with an expenditure of 300 or more shells in the process, almost walked into the German lines, was gassed, in short had a hell of a time—'you bet your life' " (Diary, October 2, 1918). For Traub's House testimony see *Losses of Thirty-Fifth Division during the Argonne Battle,* February 17, 45; February 20, 68–69. His best account of his frontline visits was p. 69: "As soon as they commenced bracketing I sized up the situa-

tion. You have to do some quick thinking under those conditions; even a major general has to think once in a while. I at once zigzagged, and I had not gotten more than 10 yards when a shell came down where I had been. Then they commenced again to try to bracket me on the new zigzagging, this chap in the air at the same time sprinkling me with machine-gun bullets. They sent a shell 15 yards to the left, and then they sent one 15 yards to the right, and then they sent another 15 yards to the left, and then another 15 yards to the right. I said, 'Old sport, get busy.' I zigzagged to the left, and I had no more than done that when a high explosive shell came down. I made one mistake. The Boche was not as stupid as I thought he was, or they may have missed the count, because they did the bracketing only once that time, and the third time caught me unprepared. The shell landed within 2 1/2 feet of me, to my left rear, and out of the 300 shells they wasted on me, that was the only dud, and it never exploded. That is the reason I am here talking to you right now."

21. Kenamore, *From Vauquois Hill to Exermont*, 204.

22. "Suggested changes in the First Army's report, correspondence with Col. G. C. Marshall, Jr.," box 14, Drum papers, especially letters of September 27, 1919, and February 24, 1920.

Contemporary Analysis

1. "Notes on Recent Operations," November 20, 1918, 235.50.1, box 16, Thirty-fifth Division historical, entry 1241, RG 120.

Sources

The place to begin any study of the battle of Meuse-Argonne is with the standard books about American participation in World War I, 1917–1918, and here the authors and editors come easily to mind: Daniel R. Beaver, Larry I. Bland, Edward M. Coffman, James Lawton Collins Jr., James A. Cooke, Harvey A. DeWeerd, John S. D. Eisenhower, Thomas Fleming, James E. Hewes Jr., D. Clayton James, Allan R. Millett, Timothy E. Nenninger, Joseph E. Persico, Forrest C. Pogue, Donald Smythe, and David F. Trask. For an introduction to this literature the best resort is the books by Russell F. Weigley on the history of the U.S. Army and on its strategy and policy.

Two books published in 1919 set out the chastening experience of the Thirty-fifth Division in the Meuse-Argonne: Clair Kenamore's *From Vauquois Hill to Exermont: A History of the Thirty-Fifth Division of the United States Army* (St. Louis: Guard) and Charles B. Hoyt's *Heroes of the Argonne: An Authentic History of the Thirty-Fifth Division* (Kansas City: Hudson). For regiments see Kenamore's *The Story of the 139th Infantry* (St. Louis: World, 1920); James E. Rieger, "139th Infantry A.E.F.–Fourth Missouri Infantry," in *History of the Missouri National Guard* (n.p.: Missouri National Guard, 1934), 207–40; Evan A. Edwards, *From Doniphan to Verdun: The Official History of the 140th Infantry* (Lawrence, Kans.: World, 1920); also William S. Triplet, *A Youth in the Meuse-Argonne: A Memoir, 1917–1918,* ed. Robert H. Ferrell (Columbia: University of Missouri Press, 2000), which tells the story of the 140th Infantry. The 129th Field Artillery Regiment appears in Jay M. Lee, *The Artilleryman: The Experiences and Impressions of an American Artillery Regiment in the World War* (Kansas City:

Spencer, 1920). Robert L. Carter's *Pictorial History of the 35th Division in the World War* (Kansas City: n.p., 1933) is a thin book with blurry photographs. The German side appears in Hermann von Giehrl, "Battle of the Meuse-Argonne," *Infantry Journal* 19 (August 1921): 131–38, and "The A.E.F. in Europe, 1917–1918," *Infantry Journal* 20 (March 1922): 292–303; also Norman S. Hall and Sigrid Schultz, "Five Red Days: The True Story of the 35th Division in the Meuse-Argonne Battle," *Liberty,* 4, no. 2 (May 14, 1927): 9–14. For machine guns see W. L. Schrantz, "Initial Machine-Gun Barrage, 35th Division, Meuse-Argonne Offensive," *Infantry Journal* 16 (November 1919): 367–71; and Donald D. Hay, "Machine Guns, 35th Division, Meuse-Argonne Operation, Sept. 26–Oct. 1, 1918," *Infantry Journal* 40 (May–June 1933): 193–206.

A miscellany, but a fascinating one, appears in the three groups of congressional hearings: *Losses of Thirty-Fifth Division during the Argonne Battle,* hearings before the Committee on Rules, House of Representatives, January 24, February 17, 18, 1919 (Washington, D.C.: Government Printing Office, 1919); *American Troops at the Argonne,* hearings before the Committee on Military Affairs, February 18, 22, 1919, U.S. Senate, 65th Cong., 3rd sess. (Washington, D.C.: Government Printing Office, 1919); *Army Appropriation Bill, 1920,* hearing before the Committee on Military Affairs, February 20, 1919, U.S. Senate, 65th Cong., 3rd sess. (Washington, D.C.: Government Printing Office, 1919).

In the early 1940s the U.S. Army published a series of pamphlets on divisions in the AEF, and that for the Thirty-fifth (Washington, D.C.: American Battle Monuments Commission, 1944) contains a splendid large-scale map of the Thirty-fifth's sector. Edward P. Rankin Jr., *The Santa Fe Trail Leads to France: A Narrative of Battle Service of the 110th Engineers in the Meuse-Argonne Offensive* (Kansas City: Richardson, 1933), has a large-scale map of the engineers' line of that regiment within the Thirty-fifth Division.

The two prime manuscript depositories for the Thirty-fifth Division, and for the entire U.S. Army in World War I, are the U.S. Army Military History Institute, a part of the Army War College at Carlisle Barracks, Carlisle, Pennsylvania; and the National Archives in College Park, Maryland, a huge new glass-enclosed structure formerly known as Archives II (the Archives building of the 1930s at Seventh and Pennsylvania in Washington, D.C., is now only for military records prior to the year 1900 and for genealogical research in immigration and other records). The Military History Institute at Carlisle has two principal files, one by name and the other by unit. The name file dates into the military past, with more recent additions, and is worth going through by computer check for 1917–1918. Papers pertaining to the Thirty-fifth Division are notably those of Hugh A. Drum and Dennis E. Nolan. The unit file—General Headquarters (GHQ), army, corps, division, brigade, regiment, battalion, company or battery— consists mostly of material accumulated by the so-called survey, a massive mailing of questionnaires to veterans that began shortly after the institute opened and gathered not merely answers to the questionnaires but, of much more value, diaries and memoirs and letters. The diaries are the best part of the survey, the memoirs the next best, and the letters usually of slight value because of censorship.

At least equal to the holdings of the institute are papers of the AEF, and within them the Thirty-fifth, gathered and easily available in the National Archives. A researcher initially has a feeling of overwhelming mass, that there is far too much material to read or even look at, but it is manageable if the researcher is willing to spend the time. A few days will not suffice for anything beyond random impressions. The first recourse must be to archivists of the Modern Military Branch—for World War I the branch chief, Timothy Nenninger, and the specialist for World War I, Mitchell Yockelson. They will point out files for each division in the AEF. For the Missouri-Kansas division the file known as "Thirty-fifth Division historical" consists of twenty-two Hollinger boxes, each five inches or so wide, in which papers are filed vertically. After the war army archivists organized division papers by a decimal system that begins with histories and passes to units—infantry brigades and regiments, the artillery brigade and its regiments, the engineer regiment, machine-gun and signal battalions, and trains. Beyond the historical files the resources are General Headquarters (GHQ), army, and corps files. Army files are those of First Army and Second Army. The latter became operative in mid-October. For special files see those of inspectors for General Headquarters, army, and corps, also G-3 (operations) and G-5 (training). Seeking to obtain correct versions of what happened in the war, the Battle Monuments Commission during the 1920s accumulated much material of interest, with input not merely by army specialists but also by participants; the commission papers are in a separate file, by division.

Manuscripts in state historical societies can be helpful, although in regard to the Thirty-fifth Division the State Historical Society of Missouri at Columbia and the Missouri Historical Society in St. Louis do not possess much of interest. The Harry S. Truman Library in Independence contains papers of Ralph E. Truman, intelligence officer of the 140th Infantry Regiment, and of course those of his first cousin, the later president, captain of Battery D, 129th Field Artillery Regiment, Sixtieth Field Artillery Brigade. Papers of Brigadier General Charles I. Martin, commanding the Seventieth Infantry Brigade until just before the opening of the Meuse-Argonne, are in the Kansas State Historical Society in Topeka.

A special repository of records, as well as the finest collection of World War I artifacts in the United States, is the Liberty Memorial in Kansas City, with two magnificent art-deco galleries and a tower, with research rooms below, erected by public subscription in the 1920s and newly refurbished. It has a large and enlarging collection of books, pamphlets, and manuscripts pertaining to the Thirty-fifth Division.

Index